Nightingale Watch
A Journey of Animal Ministry

Michele Rinaldi

Table of Contents

Dedication

This book is dedicated to all the animals that have entered my life and given so much love and trust to me. I have been privileged to experience their purity and goodness. I am a better person for it.

A special dedication is made in memory of Lynn, my friend, mentor and supporter. Her love for animals and generosity was unequalled. Thanks for all of it, Lynn.

Acknowledgments

I wish to thank each and every family member, friend, and fellow advocate for their ever-present support of my work throughout the years. Your belief in me has never wavered and has only strengthened and validated my mission to protect and care for all living creatures.

My collaboration with Western Publishing House has been instrumental in providing both guidance and direction in my journey to become an author. Harvey West and her team have been the driving force in eliciting talents I didn't even know I had. My deepest gratitude to Harvey for her steady presence, encouragement and belief in me. Thank you as well to my newest muse, Emma.

I would be remiss not to cite a few of the exceptional authors, scientists, anthropologists that I have studied. Henry Beston, Reverend Hammond, Oliver Sachs, Carl Safina, Albert Schweitzer, Max Lucada and Jane Goodall serve as standard bearers for enrichment and growth. Everything I assimilated from their writings coalesced into my personal foundation of beliefs, discoveries and reflections. It is an honor to present my work as a testament to them.

Sincere gratitude to my library/IT "Dream Team": Joel, Liju, and Sajan, for their selfless assistance.

A special thank you to my dear friends and cheering section, Pam, Sharon, Vicki and Sue. My deepest thanks to Pam, although many miles apart has fueled my dream with her voice of reason, support and shared faith.

Thank you, Sharon for your presence as an exceptional employee who emerged a friend. Always willing to help me in my adventures and having fun on the way.

My heartfelt thanks to my longtime friend, Vicki. Thanks for the laughs, the "squabbles" and memories. Through all the ups and downs you have stayed loyal and been there to lend an ear and your heart.

I am beyond grateful to Sue (aka Goobs) for it all. It seems there was never a time you were not there. Personal assistant, co- worker, confidant and my constant fan. My work and this book defines our friendship.

Thank you all for a lifetime of friendship, unwavering support and love that has carried me through every season of this odyssey.

About the Author

Michele has worked for close to 40 years in the veterinary and animal welfare field. Prior to this, she taught special education and later served as a principal. Her desire to care for animals led her to pursue veterinary nursing, specializing in intensive care and internal medicine. Over time, her focus shifted to hospice and palliative care, where her dedication remains to this day.

For the better part of her adult life, Michele's work has centered on helping others, beginning with her role in special education. Her career path eventually pivoted toward veterinary and animal welfare, where she found a deep sense of purpose. She considers herself fortunate to be on this journey of animal ministry. Based in the New York Hudson Valley, Michele has cared for a wide variety of animals in a region rich with wildlife and natural beauty.

Her connection with these animals, along with fellow animal advocates, has been a continuing source of inspiration. She invites readers to explore these "tails" and share in the oneness and passion that define her work.

Prologue

Imagine being someone who stops to pick up a snapping turtle sitting in the road, risking a serious bite to help it cross safely. Or assisting another person in catching their dog as it frantically runs back and forth along the median of the Garden State Parkway. Is it feasible for someone to care for an ill swan by hand-feeding it? Or to help an injured Canada goose that can't fly by throwing food onto the river and ice to ensure its survival?

Do you think a person would stop traffic on the Merritt Parkway—blocking two lanes—to guide a confused and lost goose to safety as it wanders in traffic, its mate lying dead on the side of the road?

Well, allow me to introduce myself—simply as someone who has been privileged to devote nearly forty years to animals. Their care and protection have been both my vocation and my passion, as a veterinary technician, hospital manager, wildlife rehabilitator, and animal shelter director.

I have witnessed moments that made my heart soar, as well as actions that reveal the darker side of humanity. It is said that love comes at a high price, but I have found it to be well worth the cost. My education, in a sense, has been shaped and enriched by the reflections and writings of extraordinary individuals such as Oliver

Sacks, Albert Schweitzer, religious leaders and pastors of all faiths, anthropologists like Jane Goodall, and writers such as Henry Beston and Carl Safina.

I invite you to meet the many living creatures I have had the privilege of sharing time and space with—and I hope you enjoy the journey as much as I have.

Part One: Rescue

Dottie

"The Eyes Are Windows to the Soul"

This is Dottie's story—her time in a shelter under trying circumstances, to say the least. With that being said, I invite you to share in the triumph of Dottie, who was not only blind but also a "senior" at approximately 14 years of age.

Blind cats and dogs are often termed "special needs," but we prefer to think of them as "other-abled" companions who, despite their disabilities, can be active, loving, and devoted.

Dottie's life had been rocky from the very beginning. She was living on the periphery of a feral colony, clearly not integrated into the group, when she was trapped. Upon arrival at the shelter, she quickly settled in, demonstrating friendliness and affection toward people.

Around three months later, she was diagnosed with glaucoma. Her right eye became detached, requiring removal. Dottie struggled to adjust to this trauma and became timid and frightened. Glaucoma had already stolen the vision in one eye and then, just as insidiously staked a foothold in her left eye. Unfortunately, that eye also had to be removed, plunging her into total darkness with little time to adapt to her terrifying new world.

Dottie was deeply challenged by her sightless existence. When taken out of her cage, she became defensive, perhaps as a means of self-protection. Yet, in the comfort of her "condo" cage, she responded to her name and loved being petted. At times, however, she would retreat into a corner, seeking solitude.

As a stray, Dottie had exemplified survival of the fittest. Now, her disability forced her to retreat into the safety of isolation. Yet, despite all she had endured, a glimmer of hope remained steadfast. Her trust in human contact was not erased—only hidden.

Dottie teaches us the true meaning of "going with the flow." Her genuine personality was never bound by blindness. While her youth had faded, her capacity to love and be loved remained undiminished. Blindness would not stand in the way of her chance to find a home.

Dottie is tough.

Dottie has resilience.

Dottie is capable.

Dottie is strong.

Above all, Dottie is a survivor. She teaches us valuable lessons, and she lived life on her own terms.

The adage "the eyes are the window to the soul" takes on a different meaning here. You did not need to look into Dottie's eyes to see her soul—she had the uncanny ability to reach into yours and embrace your heart.

Dottie spoke volumes. What did she say? Simply that she wanted one last chance—to live out her final years in a warm, quiet home where she would be cherished and doted upon. She would thrive in a place where she was the sole recipient of unadulterated pampering.

Dottie was deeply loved at the shelter by staff and volunteers alike. Still, we feared she might never find a home.

But then, she did.

Dottie was adopted by a loving, caring couple—senior citizens who fell in love with her. Her remaining years were filled with love, security, and safety—and, I would venture to say, joy.

She passed away at home, and I truly believe that, at last, she was finally able to say:

"I once was lost, but now am found; was blind, but now I see."

—Amazing Grace

Reflections on Seeing

The gifts of humans and animals indeed overlap. While we live side by side with animals, the question arises: Who is the teacher, and who is the student?

Dottie's blindness and resilience highlight our own blindness. How can we emulate her inner sight—her love, strength of spirit, and unconditional kindness—when so often, all we see is a world filled with despair, sorrow, and hurt?

We, like our animal companions, carry invisible backpacks—burdens unseen by the eyes. Dottie was blind, yet she fought to see joy, love, and survival. Her baggage was light and diaphanous, while ours can sometimes feel like heavy boulders.

Let us open our eyes to love, sincerity, and respect, and wear them as a mantle. Let our own blindness, like Dottie's, reveal the very essence of our souls and affirm our shared existence.

Ben

"Age is Only a Number in Dog Years"

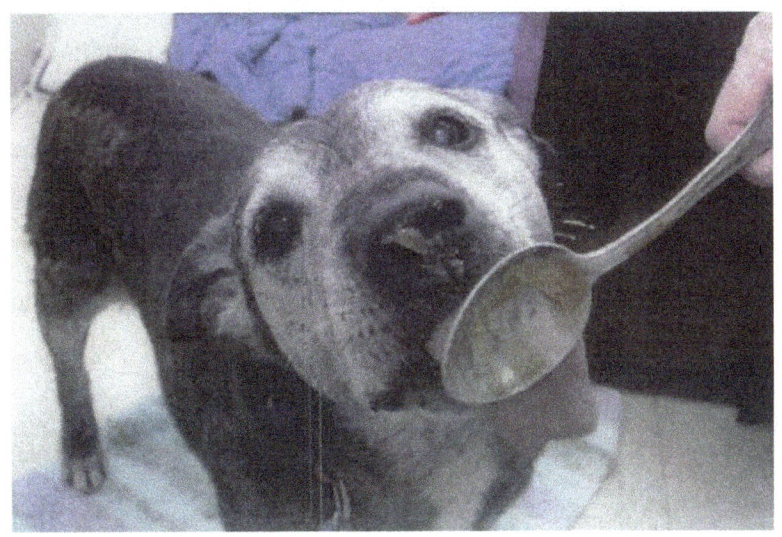

When you reach your golden years or if you're already there you will surely long for comfort, security, peace, and, most of all, love. You won't dwell on past achievements or failures; instead, you'll embrace each day as a gift, no matter the number.

I like to believe the same applies to senior pets. However, unlike us, they are not burdened with worry or regret over their past. They live in the moment, unaware of their age—perhaps a bit slower, but no less present. It is often said that "youth is wasted on the young," but perhaps that sentiment belongs to animals as well. Age is not a limitation for them but a testament to their resilience. It is a gift of hope, time, and respect—a promise of continuity with their owner and with God.

With that in mind, let me introduce Ben, a 9-year-old Akita/Shepherd mix. He was brought to the shelter after being surrendered by his owners. Why? They simply could not—or chose not to—fulfill their responsibility to an aging dog.

One look at Ben, and your gaze would be drawn to his eyes. You couldn't resist. This gentle giant revealed a wise and loving soul through that window. Ben was completely at ease in his own skin (a lesson we could all learn). He was unassuming, content, and undemanding. I imagine his definition of heaven was snoozing on an oversized plush bed, taking leisurely outdoor strolls, and having his stash of toys within easy reach.

How did Ben manage to stay perpetually young? Simply by responding to love. A gentle pet or a warm hug was all he needed, yet what he gave back in return was immeasurable. There is a television commercial that should have been dedicated to him and all senior pets: "Unconditional love, enduring devotion, a faithful friend… priceless!"

Ben was adored by the shelter staff, but he had yet to meet his forever family. Then, a middle-aged couple visited. They were taken with Ben but hesitant about his age. In addition to being a senior dog, Ben had chronic dermatological issues requiring regular treatment, as well as a costly special diet.

It was clear that the couple had fallen under his spell, but they were unprepared for the financial responsibility of his medical care. The shelter, recognizing what a great loss this would be for Ben, proposed a solution: The couple could foster him while the shelter continued to cover his medical expenses.

Ben did not take up much space in their home, but he instantly took over their hearts. After many months in foster care, he was formally adopted as a permanent member of their family.

Ben had a wonderful life, becoming the center of their world. He often visited the shelter with his owners. He was especially bonded to the husband, and the feeling was undoubtedly mutual.

As time went on, the signs of aging became more evident. His appetite diminished, and he struggled to get up and walk. The day we all dreaded arrived—not as a surprise, but as a painful, yet loving, act of mercy. It was time to let him go with dignity and deepest love.

A few days later, the husband returned to visit. Heartbroken, he vowed never to go through this again. Loving Ben and losing him had been too devastating. I told him that the depth of love he felt for Ben meant he had the capacity to love again. There were no perfect or magical words to heal his grief, but I simply said:

"Do not cry because Ben is not here smile because he was."

Reflections on Simplicity

If you're lucky, you have known—or lived with—a dog or cat who has reached their golden years. These animals enrich our lives, becoming part of our human family for as long as we are privileged to have them. They don't get to choose their owners (although I believe they know), yet they give their lives to us without question. For this gift—and all that comes with it—they deserve our love and care in the twilight of their lives.

Looking back at all the senior animals I have taken in, I remain in awe of their simplicity. As the saying goes, "what you see is what you get." In all honesty, can we say the same about ourselves? We wear masks—hiding our mistakes, selfishness, and insecurities. We get caught in webs of guilt, worry, anger, and disappointment. Sometimes, these emotions feel overwhelming, and we just want to throw up our hands and scream, "Enough of this absurdity!"

Now, take Ben—nothing about him was false. He simply lived in the moment. He was not burdened by the past or anxious about the future. He didn't hold grudges, he didn't lose sleep over unkind words. Like water off a bird's back, he moved through life with his soul exposed—no more, no less. The most monumental thing he did? He was grateful. Grateful for food, a home, and love—expressed with one big, sloppy, wet kiss.

Wouldn't it be a blessing for all of us to emulate these wondrous creatures? To be thankful for a roof over our heads, food on the table, and someone to love us?

If we could truly live in the moment, we would be intimately and lovingly connected to all the Bens in the world. Neither we nor they know when our time on this earth will end. Let us live in gratitude for each day, embracing it as a blessing in our shared journey.

For here and now, we are the recipients of a lick on the face, a soothing purr, and a warm cuddle—expressions of unconditional love. In return, let us extend our love to all living creatures, sending forth boundless prayers for their protection and care.

Emily Ann

"French Fries & Emily"

Sometimes, I close my eyes and revisit my pets that have passed on. The quiet silence and reflection spark an invocation. I repeat the name Emily Ann over and over again, like a chant, yet bearing a melody of its own. I conjure up the image of Emily, and I smile so hard that my soul is uplifted.

So here begins the story of Emily—her journey of being lost and found.

The day I visited the local shelter was like any other. I had collected blankets, towels, and beds for the dogs waiting to be found, so to speak.

My intent was meaningful, but bearing witness to their surroundings always tore at my heart. I passed each dog run, amidst the cacophony of barking, whining, and cries. I couldn't help but think that the cement floor served as their bed, the cage fencing as their lair, and the dim lighting as their only reality. Man-made dungeons surrounded me, each with a towel or blanket placed as a token gesture of supposed humanity—both unforgiving and unyielding.

As I passed one particular run, I noticed something at the very end, barely visible in the darkness. I couldn't quite distinguish what it was. I asked a staff member, who told me it was a female dog found wandering the streets. She was not groomed or cared for in any respect. She had cataracts and was blind, estimated to be around 15 years old. They would wait three days for her to be claimed. If no one came for her, she was to be euthanized.

Not even a New York second passed between hearing their plan and making my decision. Anyone could see the odds were against her. Just another dog lost, abandoned, dumped—tossed aside as no longer useful.

After battling with the staff member, I convinced him of my resolve to care for her. He carried her out of the run and presented her to me. I held this little creature, and my heart broke. To think her life was so trivialized...

She appeared to be a Yorkshire Terrier mix, weighing about 15 pounds. Her sparse, matted coat barely covered her frail body. Her cataract-clouded eyes, warts, and scar tissue bore witness to a hard life. She shivered in my arms, and as I held her, I felt her lean into me.

At that moment, I knew.

I would protect her.

We would rise above the inequalities she had faced.

She became Emily Ann, the survivor.

It didn't take long for Emily to settle into her new home. She explored her surroundings, bumping into objects along the way. She was also incontinent, so every day, I laid out several sheets for her, creating a washable bed.

From the moment I met her, she made me laugh. Her bedding became a ritual. She would find the sheets on the floor, spin in circles, and paw at them as if "fluffing" them just right. Only when she was satisfied would she plop down for a nap.

Emily didn't hear well, but somehow, she always recognized my voice. She, on the other hand, was never shy about vocalizing. She barked persistently when it was time to eat, time to go out, or time to be picked up. Her sharp, steady barks carried a confidence far bigger than her size. I called it her "yappy" voice.

Now, don't let Emily's small stature fool you—she was a curmudgeon at heart.

Because her coat was so sparse, I bought her a turtleneck sweater for warmth. Dressing her was an event in itself. As soon as I pulled the sweater over her head and got her feet through, she would squirm and grunt. If particularly annoyed, she'd snap at the air as though it were her persecutor. Once freed from the sweater, she would shake her entire body so vigorously that she sometimes lost her balance and toppled over just to make sure I knew exactly how much she despised it.

Sweaters were bad enough. But kisses? Unacceptable.

Whenever I kissed her, she would wiggle her head back and forth in a desperate attempt to escape. If she could have spoken, I'm certain she would have protested about the indignity of it all!

Now, we come to Emily's happy legacy hence the title of this story.

Whenever I came home and found her sleeping, I avoided calling or touching her, fearing I'd startle her out of a deep sleep.

But one particular day, I walked in carrying French fries from a local fast-food place. I quietly sat down, watching Emily as she slept.

Then, without warning, she sat up, her snout straight in the air, sniffing with intensity.

She got up and, with impressive determination, followed the scent straight to me.

Of course, I shared my fries with her.

From that day forward, French fries became her special treat—and her personal wake-up alarm.

Oh, you silly girl, Emily.

Emily's life with me was a blessing—for me, and for her. For two more years, she had a safe home, warmth, and love.

Then, one day, I found her lying in her bed, caught in the throes of one grand mal seizure after another. They came relentlessly, merging into one.

I rushed her to the emergency vet hospital.

The doctor and I quickly understood the gravity of the situation.

Her eyes were open, but her pupils were fixed. She did not respond to my voice or touch.

We didn't know exactly when the seizures had begun, but we did know one thing: Emily was not coming back from this.

The neurological damage was most likely severe.

And so, I let her go.

No longer lost.

She had found her way home.

Reflections on Lost and Found

There are several definitions of the term lost, one of which resonates deeply with Emily and all others like her both domestic and wild. One can be lost in terms of physical surroundings, without a home, but more profoundly, one can be lost from love no longer held, no longer seen, no longer heard.

Those who are broken and abused sometimes survive through sheer strength of spirit and an unwavering love for humans.

Humans can be lost, too-the homeless with no place to go, robbed of hope and direction. For them, survival is a struggle, and finding a reason to live can seem impossible.

Yet, no matter the circumstances, whether human or animal, there remains a road on life's journey that leads to being found. There is a bond between us and our fellow beings—one that is spiritual, pure, and sacred. We are, indeed, our brother's keeper.

Emily, despite her many struggles, navigated her way to being found. She discovered love.

The perpetual question arises: Who rescues whom?

In being adopted, Emily found safety, respect, and a beautiful life. In return, she gave of herself—trusting, bringing laughter and magic into the lives around her. She became a standard-bearer for hope and a living example of eternal love and resilience.

Humans sometimes need a roadmap to guide them out of the prison of being lost. They must seek the deeper truth—that all life is one. They must embrace companionship and trust.

To be found is to strive toward becoming better people. When you shine on the inside, that light ultimately radiates outward. Be kind, and you will find kindness. Be compassionate, and you will receive compassion. Appreciate each day as though it were your last.

I'm sure Emily lived in the moment as well.

No matter the species, being found is the resolution to being lost.

We all lose pieces of ourselves along the way, but in the end, we share a mutual existence that transcends the physical world.

So start by giving away some of your French fries!

Ginny

"Chicken Dance"

I have witnessed countless animals relinquished to shelters under various circumstances. In the end, these creatures are victims of abandonment. This is not to say that judgment should be passed on their owners. It is not our right to indict people simply because we disagree with their decisions. Life brings unexpected challenges with dramatic consequences. What if the owner dies? What if they lose their home or job? The list is endless, but the focus must always be the animal, not the reason they were given up.

Ginny's story seemed to have the odds stacked against her from the very beginning. She was a chubby Boston Terrier mix, already advanced in years. Her owner, a senior citizen, found himself financially and physically unable to care for her any longer. Family members did not feel comfortable taking responsibility. Let's go back to my initial thought on blame and judgment and simply say—no judgment.

What I knew, without a shadow of a doubt, was that Ginny needed a home. And that was all that mattered.

Ginny adapted surprisingly well to her new circumstances. Her new home was not a kennel, but a private suite in my office. However, I had a feeling she had underlying medical issues, so I wasted no time getting an assessment from our veterinarian. I also reached out to the owner's daughter, who elaborated as best she could on Ginny's history.

Test results confirmed my instincts—Ginny was terminally ill with cancer. Euthanasia was dismissed, at least for the time being, based on her energy levels, appetite, and overall spirit. She was still full of life, and that was all the reason I needed to foster her.

Ginny walked into my house without missing a beat. I was curious about how she would react to my neurologically impaired cat, Brook. To my relief, they hit it off immediately—no fights, no tension, just a calm coexistence.

Ginny was on pain medication, which helped significantly, but I had to be gentle when picking her up, as her underbelly was extremely sensitive. The same care was required when cleaning her after she went outside.

Despite her limitations and discomfort, Ginny embodied pure joy. She had an instinctive bond with me from the start. Whenever I came home, she would rush to the door, so animated, as if I had been gone for years. Her innocence was practically tangible, and at times, she was downright comical.

One particular moment still makes me laugh. One day, I knew I would be out for a while, and I wasn't sure how Ginny and Brook would interact alone. So, I placed a dog pen gate around the area where Ginny was sleeping, keeping them separated while still allowing them to see each other.

Now you have to keep in mind, Brook's difficulty with walking. When I returned home and opened the front door, I laughed so hard I nearly cried. Not only was Ginny exactly where I had left her, but Brook was right besides her—looking completely mystified as to how she had ended up there. It was absolutely priceless!

Ginny didn't demand much to be happy—except for one thing: chicken.

Roasted chicken, grilled chicken, Kentucky Fried—if it was chicken, she wanted it. It didn't take long to realize just how enthusiastic she was about her favorite food.

All I had to do was say, *"Do you want your chicken?"* and she would bounce up and down on her front legs, jitterbugging on her back ones. She had an uncanny ability to make me laugh out loud. It wasn't long before she associated my arrival with her favorite treat. The moment I walked through the door, she would run to me, eagerly anticipating her beloved chicken.

And just like that, the chicken dance took on a whole new meaning.

Aside from her love for chicken, Ginny adored sunbathing. It was summertime, and she would lay on a blanket on the porch, looking utterly regal, without a care in the world.

It was then that I truly realized—a little can mean a lot.

Ginny taught me well.

She had settled in easily, danced her dance and enjoyed life's

Simple joys.

She lived the remainder of her life with few demands. She was loving, affectionate, and found a comforting sense of home with me. We were good together, and she was happy.

Our time was painfully short.

Ginny lived in the moment, expecting nothing but love, and giving so much more in return. The bond we shared was delicate, yet full of life—so perfect that it felt almost too pure for this world.

She remained with me for two more months. Though brief, it was enough for her to leave her unique mark on this world. In that time, she was no longer my foster dog—she had become family.

Even now, I smile unabashedly when I think of her—practically grinning back at me.

All bets are on Ginny performing the best chicken dance in heaven.

Reflections on Creature Comforts

For the most part, humans are creatures of habit, striving to attain all sorts of creature comforts. But why do we seek external things to feel better and gratified?

Let's look at Ginny as a companion. Her needs were simple and instinctive—food, water, and a place to sleep. We, on the other hand, chase after big bank accounts, luxury cars, and the nicest houses in the neighborhood. The difference lies in the simplicity of fulfillment. Here was an animal that thrived on one essential thing—not an object, but a feeling.

The love and companionship of a human was Ginny's ultimate comfort. She had to go no further than inside herself to find peace. The harsh reality was the inevitability of her death, but she didn't know that—just as we don't know when our own passing will occur. She didn't worry about why am I not with my owner? Will I stay with my new family? What will tomorrow bring?

For Ginny, there was no tomorrow—only today.

She lived, as we have learned, one day at a time. She simply was. Her energy, innocence, and trust were freely and generously gifted to me. And her greatest reward was my love.

Humans need to spend more time looking within rather than exhausting themselves chasing inconsequential desires. You'll work out more to be admired. You'll adopt better eating habits to show off your progress. You'll learn new skills to impress others. While these goals may start with good intentions, they often fall short of what truly matters.

They don't necessarily make you better people—or role models.

Take a step back and examine your intentions. So your pants are a little tight? Buy elastic. Can't run a 5K? Take a brisk walk instead. The point is this: when you shine on the inside, you ultimately shine outwardly.

Be kinder. Be more compassionate. Respect others—including animals.

If we hope to find true happiness, we should take a lesson from Ginny's life. Welcome each day as a gift. Today's joy and companionship should be enough. Don't waste time dwelling on the past. Should haves and could haves did not exist for Ginny.

Instead of being haunted by regrets, replace them with a love so great that it spills over into your community—toward both humanity and all living creatures.

I think of Ginny often, and every time, I feel a smile coming on. I was privileged to have had her company and love. She was my teacher, and I learned well.

Her journey, like ours, was a road she had to travel.

Take every opportunity to travel that path with an open heart—and share in the joy of truly living and loving.

Part Two: Redemption

Beth and Katie

"Newport Girls"

Newport, Rhode Island—a place of luxury and charm. Surrounded by water on all sides, it offers welcoming hospitality and the beauty of a time gone by.

In my opinion, as a loyal vacationer for the last ten years, I can attest to a diamond in the rough called the Potter League. This animal shelter stands among the best and has been finding homes for animals for 95 years. Most tourists enjoy their share of shopping, sightseeing, and dining, but I, for one, always made a visit to the Potter League the first stop on my itinerary.

Whenever I visited, I made a point of meeting senior or disabled cats. That's how I was introduced to Beth. On one tour, a staff member brought me to an open room with about five older cats. Beth—who would come to be known by that name—caught my eye immediately, though I couldn't explain why. By most standards, she wasn't a beauty. A little rough around the edges, worn-looking, thin and lanky. While the other cats interacted with each other, Beth was a loner. She was curled up in a small cat condo, with only her face visible. Her only interaction was a swat with her front paw at anyone who passed by.

I was allowed to go into the room and spend time with her. She really didn't want any part of me. Surprisingly, she graced me with a swat as well. Eventually, she came over and simply sat near me. I immediately sensed a sadness or emptiness in Beth. Beyond her curmudgeonly behavior, the word that came to mind was lost.

Later, the staff told me she had belonged to an elderly woman who had fallen ill. Beth was sent to live with the woman's son, but unexpectedly, he passed away. Her former owner was too sick to take her back, so Beth was surrendered to the Potter League. She had been there quite a while with little or no interest from the public.

I tried to trust my instincts, but this interaction with her was so much more. All interactions are destined, not accidents and put into motion for a reason. Beauty and charm weren't her bargaining chips, yet she pulled me in. I felt a gentleness and tranquility in her that needed to be touched and awakened.

Beth and I signed an adoption contract, but our soul contract was something much deeper—on another plane.

Beth came home with me the following morning, serenading me during the 3.5-hour drive with blood-curdling caterwauls. I suppose she didn't care for the radio! We arrived safely, and the other cats accepted her with an aloof sniff and a carefully chosen spot nearby. In the few years we shared, she was never aggressive or confrontational. She simply coexisted and guarded her space.

I found her comical in her own way—best described as a grouchy old lady. Yet she bore the name Beth, which conjured images of sweetness and femininity. Our bond deepened over time. One of her favorite habits was to sneak up behind me and scream like a banshee when I least expected it. It never failed to make me jump. Even at nearly 16 years old, she would see me sit down and take a flying leap into my lap. She was a bit bony, but she seemed to enjoy the cushion.

About a year after adopting Beth, I visited the shelter again. A staff member showed me around the senior section, and a striking tortoiseshell female caught my eye. She had been relinquished by owners who were moving. The league named her "Kitty" which really under-minded her beauty and personality. The staff proceeded to open the cage door and as soon as they did, Kitty literally jumped not out, but out directly into my arms. Thankfully, I was a decent catch, and she leapt like a tiger through a hoop. A very energetic connection sparked between us in that brief moment. I could tell she had spirit—and the capacity for unconditional love.

So off to New York we went, and she was newly christened Katie.

Katie was affectionate with people and other cats. She would sleep beside them, never causing conflict. The others were kind enough to tolerate her. Surprisingly, Katie was the only one Beth ever got close to. In Beth's world, "close" meant sharing the same couch, chair, or bed.

Katie had her own form of neediness—relishing being petted or picked up. She'd always sit on the arm of the chair next to me, even when Beth was on my lap. Every day with Katie was a joy. She was playful and carefree, always living in the moment. No hidden agenda—just love.

I sincerely believe that Beth and Katie, though not related, possessed grateful hearts and souls. They both touched something deep within me that needed to be touched. They helped me speak to their souls and spirits. Whatever was lost, damaged, or forgotten, they helped each other heal—and reached out to help me heal too.

Katie and Beth both passed away from kidney failure in the same year, just one month apart.

Safe journey, my forever Newport Girls. Ever united, ever missed, and ever loved. How blessed I was to find them.

Reflections on Homelessness

Homelessness is a multidimensional experience for both humans and animals. Neither group chooses to be homeless, especially when this reality is shaped by factors beyond their control. Prejudice, discrimination, insults, and more have long been directed at homeless individuals. Today, alternative terms like unsheltered or houseless have emerged in an effort to shift perception.

There are an estimated 70 million dogs and cats struggling with little or no resources to survive. They, too, become homeless through circumstances not of their choosing. Many are lost, abandoned, abused, or surrendered to shelters. There is no polite way to put it: they are tossed aside like yesterday's news.

Homelessness is not simply the absence of a residence. It is the condition of being unseen, forgotten. It reflects a deeper, often ignored reality—that those who are suffering, whether on the street or in a shelter cage, often go unnoticed. It's as if they don't exist. Are they too old, too unsightly, and too needy? Perhaps some would say yes. But all of them have needs that transcend physical appearance. They yearn to be acknowledged, valued, and loved.

Beth and Katie were often passed by because of how they looked or behaved. How could anyone know they were silently reaching out, desperate to escape their isolation? They wanted companionship, attention, and a sense of worth that comes from being loved. Eventually, they were given a chance to be part of a family and to experience appreciation and connection. Humans are no different. How often do we wonder if anyone sees our loneliness? Do we wait for someone to tell us we're okay, that we're worthy? Do we still carry hope that love is out there?

The lesson we learn from animals is their extraordinary ability to fill the emotional gaps in our lives. And the cost? Just one thing—love and comfort in return. They are gifted in providing meaning, no matter who we are. Regardless of your faith, occupation, financial status, or even your housing situation, everyone is eligible for a win-win reward.

The most powerful example of this lies with unhoused individuals who possess almost nothing—no home, no clean clothes, no hygiene products, sometimes not even food. Yet, even in the depths of hardship, they whisper a silent plea: to be seen, to be accepted, to be befriended. For them, caring for a Beth or a Katie is not just companionship—it is proof that they matter. That they are important. That they are loved.

Girlie Girl / Handsome Boy

"Wild Thing, You Make My Heart Sing"

I was introduced to the life of feral cats shortly after my move to a residence on the Hudson. My community had its share of "strays," but I soon discovered that, in fact, most of them were feral. These cats had no particular interest in bonding with me. I, in fact, represented one thing: food. From their perspective, human = food = good.

Specifically, there were two male cats, most assuredly at the pinnacle of the feline hierarchy. I later named them Orange Boy and Handsome Boy. They were surely—lords of the manor.

Handsome Boy was commanding, to say the least. He was well-built, muscular, and stocky. He walked with confidence, and his appearance on the street felt like a royal announcement. Orange Boy walked with assurance as well, although his stride was more cautious. He had a surreptitious nature. His presence projected the silence and stealth of a hungry cat.

Both of these guys armed themselves with tough and tenacious posturing whenever they entered someone else's space. The "fur was about to fly" whenever a rumble seemed imminent. They began this courtship of sorts by circling each other, moving in a crab-like manner—sideways—with magnified intensity and a guttural, menacing screech.

I soon discovered I served no purpose as an arbitrator or referee—lest I lose a hand. Trying to interfere only made things worse. Eventually, they'd move on to another arena, and more often than not, both would stand down.

One summer, they both arrived at the house for food, clearly in distress and wounded from another fight. They each had huge abscesses on their front legs. Orange Boy seemed more tentative and deferred to Handsome Boy, letting him eat first.

In the feline world—both wild and domestic—survival is the utmost priority. Cats are very "Darwinian." What does that mean?

Simply put, they live by survival of the fittest. They mask or hide injuries, more so than dogs, for example. I witnessed this instinct firsthand with both of them.

Handsome Boy was slightly more comfortable around me than Orange Boy. Not entirely trusting, but enough to sleep or stay on my porch. I obtained antibiotics under the direction of my veterinarian and disguised them in his food. Most of the healing would be painful—his leg was swollen many times over.

Interestingly, Orange Boy demonstrated a strong survival tactic. I discovered he only came out at night and hid under my car. That's where I fed him and quietly monitored his recovery.

So, the boys and I coexisted quite well. And in all honesty, although I loved both, the first time I looked into Handsome Boy's face, I knew—he was mine.

Then, things got more interesting—and, I might add, more challenging.

I was putting food out on my front porch when I glanced over at my neighbor's house. Some of the skirting near the foundation had come loose. I thought I saw something move, but since it was daylight, I chalked it up to imagination.

Then I heard a small bang.

I looked again and saw a tiny face peeking through the opening. Much to my surprise—or perhaps dismay—a petite, diminutive cat slowly emerged. I guessed she was a female, which proved to be correct. She also appeared young, perhaps one or two years old.

She was timid, not at all aggressive, and absolutely beautiful with a long, gray-beige coat. It goes without saying—we had a romantic foray in the making.

I called her "Girlie Girl" because her appearance was so delicate and domestic. She would approach the boys and try to saddle up next to them, only to be rebuffed with the swat of a paw! But for some inexplicable reason, she quickly bonded with Handsome Boy and he didn't seem to mind.

Every time you looked, they were together.

To this day, I vividly remember the moment that captured their bond. One afternoon, Girlie Girl was sitting at the bottom of the stairs on my front porch, looking up toward the top of the street. Suddenly, Handsome Boy turned the corner and began walking toward us.

She shot off like a flash and ran to meet him. He continued walking but gently butted heads with her in greeting.

I'm not a betting person, but I'm convinced that if she could speak, she would have said, "Where have you been? I've been looking for you!"

After a period of time, several of the original feral cats died off by attrition. But more were to come, as new females began arriving on the scene. With consistent diligence—and assistance from an organization called Care for Strays—the cats were saved, literally one by one. They were trapped, neutered, and released. Once they were spayed and neutered, they never returned to our community.

Several litters, once weaned, were cared for by volunteers, fostered, and adopted. Even Girlie Girl was spayed, and both Handsome Boy and Orange Boy were neutered.

The chronicle of Orange Boy continues in what I feel is the most humane way—but let me digress for now and return to our well-established courtship.

Girlie Girl and Handsome Boy, having been spayed, neutered, and vaccinated, were now ready to embark on domestic life. I always had a spare bedroom set aside for guests both human and furry. Most of the time, the furry friends won out. I installed screen doors in the doorway so they could see me and get more comfortable coming inside. I was accepted as someone who lived in close proximity, but I certainly couldn't touch them not yet.

In the meantime, six cats remained in the community, including Orange Boy. At that time, the community management issued a mandate that these cats—and any others—be trapped again and euthanized. This was unacceptable to me. I began researching and reaching out, trying to find placements for them—and thankfully, I was successful.

By 2013, Hurricane Sandy was merciless in its onslaught. My home and those of my neighbors were all adjacent to the Hudson River. The forecast was dire, and my sole focus became complying with the mandatory evacuation order. The only barrier between my house, my cats, and the incoming surge was a seawall and a set of docks.

Somehow, I managed to place my five house cats in carriers. Then, with help from a technician friend, I re-trapped both Handsome Boy and Girlie Girl. Thankfully, my brother helped me set up cages for each and every cat. God bless him—his living room looked like a kennel.

In the end, my home along with so many others—was destroyed or totaled.

After many long weeks, I was finally able to secure a new home where I could bring all seven cats. What was I thinking? But it worked out.

As time went on, the "husband and wife," as I affectionately called them, remained inseparable. Their new room was spacious, with a couch and a large window where they could sit together. I would go in regularly just to sit with them and keep them company.

The years flew by, and they grew older. I became concerned about how I would handle medical care, especially since I still couldn't physically engage with them.

Handsome Boy eventually developed several health issues dental problems, diabetes (he became insulin dependent), and more. But curiously enough, as he grew more vulnerable, he also became more trusting. Slowly, he allowed me the privilege of caring for him eventually, I could even pick him up.

He lived to become a senior cat. After he passed, my focus shifted to Girlie Girl, who very clearly grieved. She kept to herself. I absolutely ramped up the amount of time I spent with her sitting quietly at night with a light on and the radio playing softly.

She was close to 15 years old when she passed last year. And after all those years of not being able to pet her or pick her up just like Handsome Boy she unexpectedly blessed me. For nearly a whole year before she passed, I held her, carried her, and kissed her.

With both of them gone, the loss was deep but the blessing was even greater.

They had a wonderful life, and in their own way, they chose to gift me with the touch of both their bodies and their souls. As sad as I was when I had to release them, I felt the journey of our souls and could not deny them a safe journey home!

Reflections on Unconditional Love

I think, sometimes, that every interaction we have with living creatures is a kind of narrative—a record of our misgivings, prejudices, openness, engagement, and so many unfounded beliefs.

I often ponder how—and why—Handsome Boy and Girlie Girl were able to embrace each other's companionship so naturally. There appeared to be no hesitation, no prior acknowledgment of one another, and no pre-established love. And yet, for all intents and purposes, there were no rules, no expectations. They simply existed in the present. They were being—not caught up in the before or the after.

Animals are not suffocated by the trappings of materialism or power. They don't live by special terms or conditions.

If we, as humans, could walk with more humility, less anger, less fear—and so much more love—we might better understand what it means to live in a state of the unconditional.

Even if Handsome Boy and Girlie Girl had lived solely by their own terms, their lives would still be defined as unconditional. They survived by instinct and made choices, but never measured life in terms of, "What's in it for me?"

So how do we measure the relationship between Girlie Girl and Handsome Boy?

First, they sought each other's company. There were no demands. If he wanted to be alone, she knew not to disturb him. They shared the same food bowl and the same water dish—now that's really love. She trusted him. She stayed near when unfamiliar cats came around.

Maybe, based on the way we love our cats, we can learn to love humans the same way.

Don't take things personally. We give cats space to respond—we don't impose expectations, and neither do they. Imagine how different people might be if they received nurturing from the start, with no strings attached.

Learn to let people in. Don't push them away just because you feel unsafe.

Connections may be long or brief, but regardless of their length, they leave paw prints on the heart.

So, let's reflect on what we've learned from Girlie Girl and Handsome Boy's unconditional love:

They were constantly together—always physically close. They basked in the sun so near one another, they often looked like one cat.

They shared food bowls without conflict.

Grooming was mutual and seemed to go on forever.

You could see the love in their eyes—you knew it was real.

It seems like heaven to me:

No demands.

No expectations.

Just enjoying the love that's given to you.

So stay close to each other.

Touch. Physical closeness matters.

Sit in the sun together.

Bask in each other.

Don't worry about who grooms better.

Always share your food.

Look into each other's eyes often—it gives your insight into the strength and depth of your bond.

And when you and your partner are gone—like Girlie Girl and Handsome Boy—I believe you'll be welcomed with:

"Where have you been? I've been looking for you!"

Maggie May

"Angels, Pixie Dust & Light"

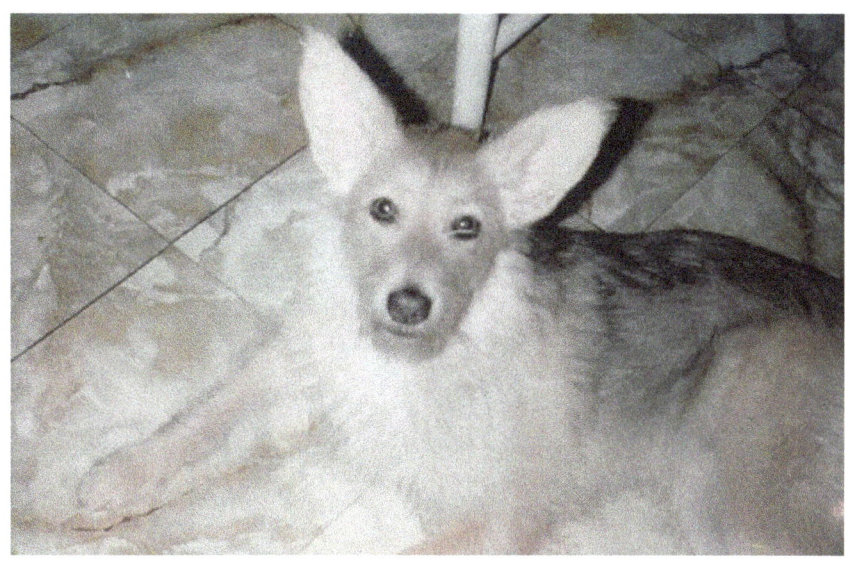

Maggie was a totally unexpected gift waiting to be claimed by me but not when I first saw her.

It all began when my best friend wanted to adopt a dog from the local shelter. We decided to visit one day, and as we were perusing the kennels, one dog practically became airborne with excitement—leaping in her run with absolute desire for contact. The staff took her out for us to meet.

Maggie was a medium-sized dog, about 30 pounds, give or take. Her coat leaned toward a terrier mix—wiry, like a bad hair day. But her standout features were her ears. It seemed that somewhere along the family tree, a German shepherd had made a surprise appearance. Up stood these ears that looked like they were meant for takeoff.

Maggie never grew into them, but she was so comical, you had no choice but to call her cute.

Thankfully, she was a medium-sized dog because she was high energy. But it was clear the energy was just pent-up—she was so happy to be outside with us.

The shelter had limited history on her, but what really surprised me was that she had been returned three times. In my wildest imagination, I couldn't understand why. Nor did the staff elaborate.

Meeting her was love at first sight. And in the spirit of following your heart, my friend threw caution to the wind and said, "Yes, to the dog!" The shelter guessed she was around two years old, and two she was—in every possible way. Maggie was the personification of a toddler. A canine whirling dervish. She leapt, jumped, and ran in circles constantly. She loved to play, tried to snuggle (barely fitting on your lap), and spread the wealth with sloppy kisses.

The story takes a step away from the joy and light after a year or two.

My best friend became ill and was hospitalized with a terminal illness. There was no family, per se, to help with Maggie's care, so I took on the responsibility. It was a somber, challenging time—especially integrating her with my cats and dogs at home. But always a ray of sunshine, Maggie thrived in her temporary home.

Three months later, my friend passed. The grief and emptiness were suffocating, but I was grateful Maggie remained resilient and, thankfully, unaware of the loss.

My role changed overnight from surrogate to adoptive mother.

Life went on. Maggie and I bonded deeply. I believed we shared a soul connection, and through that, she allowed me to feel all the gentleness, comfort, and love she had. In a way, Maggie kept my friend alive. She lived on through her, and I came to recognize that Maggie was a unique spirit who had entered my life for a reason.

As much as I have endless love for all the pets I've had, Maggie—and my cat, Brook, who you'll meet soon—were my true, singular soulmates.

Maggie and I went everywhere together. She loved car rides, curling up on the passenger seat while I ran into the store. She enjoyed walks, and I loved taking her out because everyone was immediately drawn to her. Everything she did was instinctive—she never jumped on people but happily greeted kids and adults alike, tail wagging nonstop.

In all the years I had her, I can honestly say I never heard her bark at anyone. She didn't whine or beg. Maggie was blessed with a rare gentleness and serenity. You could look into her eyes and see a light that sparkled and shone from within.

My favorite time with her was bedtime. Amidst all the others on the bed, Maggie always found her way to the front of my body as I lay on my side. And again—never a growl, never a snarl to the other pets. She simply, matter-of-factly, curled into a compact, snug ball.

Maggie lived the good life with her usual aplomb—demonstrating humor, being silly, playing with others, and did I mention making my life complete? She truly embodied my favorite character, Tinker Bell. So very "her."

But in July of 1996, the balance of life shifted ominously.

Maggie, who was always easy and undemanding, began to refuse her food. She was never a huge eater, but it was enough to notice when she didn't eat at all. One morning, as unexpected as a summer thunderstorm, she turned completely away from her food. I watched her throughout the day, and she still showed no interest the next day. Though her demeanor remained fine, I knew something was wrong.

Bloodwork confirmed what I couldn't bear to hear. My five-year-old wonder was diagnosed with acute lymphoblastic leukemia. The vet recommended palliative care. The prognosis was poor—she was already in the final stages.

Life, as I knew it, paused. I provided Maggie with round-the-clock care. I made her meals from scratch, blended smoothies, and assisted her with eating—just like the toddler she had once been. She could still walk, but I had to pick her up and place her on the couch.

How ironic that she had been so healthy, so symptomless—and now, so suddenly, she was dying. I felt buried under an avalanche of grief trying to accept it.

The disease progressed quickly. The decision was made for me when she no longer responded to her pain medication. I arranged for the vet to come to the house for the euthanasia.

Maggie had always loved being outside, so I carried her out on a warm July day. We sat together with the sun on our faces. I felt like if I hugged her any harder, she'd pass through me.

And that's exactly what she did.

When she passed, I felt her spirit move through me. She gave me a message: her soul was free, and I was still with her. She was as carefree as she had ever been. I felt a dramatic pull in my heart that told me she was well. She now wears the mantle of an angel. I sat in wonder and through my tears, I smiled.

Through my tears, I smiled. I knew that at sunrise, every soul is born again. Maggie's legacy—her loyalty, her purity—left me with some measure of divinity.

I still remember my little clown with one last moment from the vet.

There was a commercial at the time that showed scenarios of people desperately needing milk but having none, stirring up that iconic sense of FOMO (fear of missing out). The tagline was: "Got Milk?"

The vet turned to me and simply said,

"Got Maggie?"

Reflections on Beauty of Innocence

In my experience as a palliative and hospice caregiver, I have gained profound insight into the reality, surprises, and complexity of life.

The reality can be overwhelming at times, because we cling to the illusion of life lasting forever. Then, suddenly, you—or someone you love, whether human or animal—become a hospice patient, facing the inevitable end of life.

At this point, people often begin to dissect their lives. Animals, however, do not dwell on their past, nor do they worry about tomorrow. There may be no tomorrow so they live in the present. If there was ever a time to truly live in the moment, it is now.

Animals and humans share the same mystery: not knowing how long they will live. People always hope for a long life, but no one is guaranteed one of quality. To have both is, in my view, a blessing of spiritual completion.

Maggie comes to mind as a soul who shone so brightly that her light could not sustain itself for long. She was destined for a short life, but her accomplishments and qualities set a standard to be admired. Her gift to the world was simply being, her heart and soul, fully present in each moment.

Maggie was happy in every sense of the word carefree and unburdened by the need to dwell or waste time.

Humans need to do the same. That is, remember the goodness you've shared with others. Let go of regrets and guilt. Truly, truly live today as if it were your last. Hold that thought and allow yourself to embrace the truth that no one can replace you. You have lived well. You will leave a unique mark. Express yourself with the energy of your spirit.

If I have described Maggie May in a way that brings her to life for you, then know I am speaking with her voice as well.

Choose your own path. Live your life well. Die your own death. You don't have to replace Maggie—but you can walk her path.

Get excited when you see someone you love.

Show gratitude through affection.

Offer comfort with a hug.

Let others see your light, and in doing so, see themselves more clearly.

Let Maggie guide you to be an angel for others.

And don't forget to sprinkle a little fairy dust along the way to illuminate the path of humanity and remind us all of the wisdom our fellow creatures offer.

Part Three: Reverence

Pete and Gladys

"Our Swan Song"

I suppose that everyone experiences a bit of anxiety when moving, in anticipation of meeting new neighbors for the first time. I, for one, was looking forward to this, but certainly did not expect such a surprise.

As I mentioned before, my home was adjacent to a basin area or tributary of the Hudson River, and my backyard was just steps away from the docks. My neighbor across the street came over and suggested I go around to my backyard, as someone was visiting back there.

Curiosity got the best of me, and when I turned the corner, I saw two white swans swimming together near the docks. Very deliberately, I walked over—slowly and quietly so as not to frighten them. My concern soon evaporated as my better-part-of-valor approach was met with strenuous honking and hissing. My presence was an unpleasant intrusion, and so I decided to abbreviate our introduction.

Apparently, they had already decided on this as well, as they effortlessly glided away together.

Well, here I was—the new kid on the block—expecting a welcome committee with a cake or cookie, any kind of hello treasure. Instead, what did I get? My waterfowl acquaintances ignored their mute characteristic, choosing to comment with a hiss, a grunt, and "goodbye, fare thee well!"

So, I came to find out that this pair had been in the basin and outermost parts for a long time. It was estimated that they were around 18 years of age. Neighbors had dubbed them Pete and Gladys. Well, hello to my new friends—perhaps we'll pick up where we left off. I had a feeling that I was to be a third party in this remarkable romance and friendship.

Each day was graced with a visitation from Pete and Gladys. In the beginning, I stood on the docks some distance from them, simply watching and not disrupting their routine. Gradually, I was able to sit on the side and end of the dock, almost within reach of them. They observed me carefully, casting a furtive glance in my direction while still feeding and assessing my purpose there.

As time went on, their personalities started to emerge. They were an image of grace and energy, an offshoot of their pairing. Gladys set her own boundaries—slightly apart from the dock but within range of Pete. She would preen herself and command a take-charge position between Pete and me. It occurred to her that I was an interloper and she was the matriarch. Her comfort zone had not been breached by me, so for all intents and purposes, all was right with her world.

Pete, on the other hand, was quite affable. He was curious but protective of his space and his mate. I was able to reach out and sprinkle wild bird food on the water near him. When Pete was approaching, I always called him by name. He often would glide quite quickly toward me.

As with all swans, he was graceful on top but frantic underneath. There lies all the activity and paddling. His glide was as seamless as a knife going through butter—just as Gladys' movement appeared as silk shimmering on the water.

I tried to convince myself that Pete had imprinted on me, although I surely wasn't his first moving object—which would have been his mother. Just for argument's sake, we'll call it imprinting, although arguably, it was recognition of my voice and inflection.

After a long period of time—months and years—our triangle had become comfortable, non-threatening, and secure. Spending time with

Pete and Gladys was akin to slipping on a threadbare old glove: a perfect fit and a sense of being home.

Only on one occasion did I witness the behavior of Gladys and, especially, Pete as they displayed their natural instinct to protect their territory and safeguard their brood of cygnets.

This particular day, they were on the far end of the basin feeding in the wetland area when a pair of Canada Geese swam in toward the dock with goslings in tow—probably no more than a few days old. At the first sign of these unwanted trespassers, Gladys stayed fixed with her brood in the swamp area. Pete took a defensive posture, lowering his head and circling both his wings above him in a heart-shaped position.

In a split second, he began his charges—grunting and honking loudly and never letting up his speed. The female goose panicked and began to gather her brood. The babies, however, became disoriented and were paddling indiscriminately under the dock. The male goose now took on Pete's barrage of charges and attack. The goose was fighting valiantly and warding off Pete from the riverbank where the female was.

I went onto the dock and helped the goslings swim toward their mother. The two males were locked together in this life-threatening battle, yet in its own way, it was exquisite in nature. Almost... a final ballet.

All I could do was produce as much distraction and noise as possible. I equated the mutual attacks as relentless and impactful as a warship ramming a boat. The Canada goose pressed on with no pause, and Pete finally relinquished his position. As frightening as this visual was, it was a rare glimpse to witness life and death—survival of the fittest—and the protective ownership of their families.

Several years went by, and of the two, Pete was starting to decline. His feathers became more and more unkempt, and I discovered one eye to be infected with discharge. I conferred with my veterinarian, who explained there were a variety of causes: poisoning, toxins, bacteria, E. coli, etc. It was hard to treat, especially if it went systemic. The best I could do was place antibiotics in his food.

By this time, Pete trusted me enough to take food from my palm, initiating some form of palliative care. Pete had lost weight and no longer moved much around the docks. He was simply sick and old.

There was another pond about 10 minutes from my house, which often served as a refuge for the geese and swans—even Pete and Gladys.

One day, I was walking at the pond, and there on the bank was Pete, sitting with his head curled under, sleeping. I called him by name, and he looked up as I walked toward him. I asked permission in a silent prayer to be near him as I approached. I kept repeating his name and stretched out my hand to touch him. I stroked his feathers, and he never showed fear.

That moment was the final moment between Pete and me. I realized then, and still do, that it was the most intimate, magical gift he could give me—to say thank you, as I did to him.

Needless to say, I never saw Pete again. I am sure that when he passed, Gladys went off to grieve. It is reported that geese and swans mate for life, and when one is gone, the other maintains a solitary life to mourn the loss.

I, too, grieved and missed both of them, but I was privileged to have them allow me into their lives. My communion with them lives forever. Things come and go, and beauty fades—but not with them.

Legend says that a few minutes before they die, the mute swan bursts into a beautiful song. In my quiet space, I see Pete and Gladys… and oh, how wonderful—I hear them singing!

Reflections on Intersection of Souls

A Japanese legend states that two souls can be joined or intertwined by a thread that can never break or leave. There are many species that mate for life, and unless one passes away, they remain bonded and committed to each other. When animals are soul mates, they are connected in the most primal, deep interchange imaginable.

They have the same brain—basic to both them and humans. What do they feel, and why? Anxiety, pain, fear, sadness, loyalty, compassion, gratitude, and love are shared emotions. They live a shared world with humans. Pete and Gladys lived their lives in oneness, in unity, in a life born of two. All life is one, and we live side by side.

The communion of souls is the foundation for social mores, relationships, and instinctive direction. This journey enables them to survive on instinct, and in doing so, they are compelled to make choices. Observing animals in their natural world is a glimpse into their grand scheme. Communication is exponentially unified between two souls. Responsibilities such as rearing their young, working in unison, adhering to a hierarchy, and protecting from predators are essential.

Do we recognize and appreciate the nobility and beauty of living creatures? Are we capable of engaging in relationships? The question posed to us might be difficult to consider; however, the truth may be that their sharing of souls demonstrates emotions and feelings more perfectly than we.

As humans, we experience our souls intersecting or joining with another. Bear in mind that we have a strand that can—and should—be with theirs.

Let us emulate the love and divine coexistence held together by their thread. Let us step back and be generous with attitudes and actions that affirm the joining of not only souls, but minds, hearts, and spirits. What is intrinsic to animals should be to us as well.

Show unconditional love, have patience and tolerance, protect the weak and innocent. We are all one. Like Pete and Gladys, being mute does not mean being speechless. Sing a beautiful song in honor of all life—like them.

Orange Boy and the Girls

"Delaware or Bust"

As you recall, Orange Boy's life was significantly entwined with that of Girlie Girl and Handsome Boy. All of these lives converged, but took on different, permanent destinations—particularly Orange Boy. His continuing journey, as arduous as it was, protected him and literally saved his life.

I previously mentioned that the management of my community intended to trap the remaining cats and have them euthanized. Options to rescue them became increasingly difficult. There were five others besides him: a female cat and her three offspring, and another female. Although all of them were considered feral, Orange Boy and the single female had been exposed to people, whereas the other female and her kittens were highly aggressive and would be a challenge.

My work had just begun as I explored countless leads in securing a sanctuary that would accept them. My research led me to a cat sanctuary in Delaware for feral cats and/or cats that are unadoptable due to behavior. The facility is comprised of 17 acres, large buildings, barns, and other structures for the cats.

I was successful in reaching them and soon realized the opportunity might not come to fruition. The owners were reticent about accepting six ferals at once, but were willing to listen to my account of the circumstances. Their sanctuary required a two-week hold before the cats could arrive on their reserved placement date. The medical protocol was understandably stringent. All cats had to be healthy, spayed or neutered, vaccinated for rabies and distemper, and tested for FLV and FELV.

I secured a date for transport, but it didn't take long to realize how difficult the logistics were. My optimism was bordering on panic, but I kept my wits about me and persevered.

All six of my Delaware "adoptees" had to be rehoused for the preceding two weeks. Where would I place each adult and the juveniles in large dog crates? To this day, I am in deep gratitude to my two neighbors who offered spare rooms. I took full responsibility for feeding them, cleaning litter boxes and surroundings, and disposing of garbage every day—before work and after.

What a great learning curve it was to open the crate, keep them contained, withdraw and replace food, water, and litter—all as quickly as possible while litter was flying everywhere—and trying to keep my hand from getting injured. I always wanted to be a juggler or acrobat!

Another friend of mine helped me plan the trip to the sanctuary. We were aware that it would involve a 6- to 7-hour drive. I also realized that a drive this long would be stressful for them. It wasn't plausible to consider sedation, since we couldn't really get close enough to them, and food had been withdrawn to avoid vomiting.

Another crucial step was moving them from the crates to carriers. Everyone was hands-on, with no room for error. Someone had to crouch behind the back of the crate and prod them to move to the front, where another person held the carrier with its opening aligned to the crate door. Our primary goal was expediency, determination, focus— and a tremendous amount of hope in a very stressful situation.

My friends trapped all the cats with expected trepidation and old-fashioned sweat, and we loaded all the carriers into the car with a start time of 6 a.m. Mission not accomplished just yet—rather, initiated, with hopefully no speed bumps ahead.

During the course of this seemingly endless trip, we stopped and assessed everyone's status. I was met with the usual greetings of hisses and charges at the carrier doors. Behavior not in the least surprising. However, some concern centered on Orange Boy. He was crouched all the way toward the back of the carrier. He seemed very fearful and made no overt movement at all.

I got back in the car with a knot in my stomach, knowing that this trip and the separation from his home base were not going well for him. Frankly, not for me either. With a prayer in my hand, we at long last arrived at the sanctuary.

I was introduced to the staff, who explained the admission process. All of the cats would be confined in their initial building for 30 days. At the completion of the quarantine, the ferals would be evaluated and placed accordingly.

In light of this, the staff wanted to remove them from the carriers and place them in large crates. In looking at Orange Boy, I had long passed "slightly concerned." I was extremely nervous about his affect. He had his head down to the side, with his face pressed against the cage, and he was drooling a great deal.

The staff member was familiar with this type of presentation and said it was due to excessive stress—especially common in a feral. They reached out to their veterinarian, who came by in short order and suggested that Orange Boy be placed in an area far from contact with other cats and in clear visual range of the staff at all times.

At the moment, I couldn't help but feel that I had contributed to his state. Feral cats have traits and emotional characteristics that are different from domesticated cats. As I mentioned before, cats hide illness and injury from view and feel safer when they are out of sight. He had been pulled away from all familiarity and refuge and was now fully exposed and vulnerable.

I looked at him with tears streaming down my face and echoed my guilt in a prayer: I'm sorry!

The rationale behind this placement returned to me when I remembered why I had taken such action. I simply loved Orange Boy and wanted to ensure his safety. He was tough and would respond in time.

Time was moving quickly, and we needed to begin our trek home. The staff person showed me the enclosure Orange Boy would be in. It was a fenced area containing a barn with a loft upstairs. It seemed like an answer to our prayers, as he had privacy, a place to visually see his surroundings, and a comfort zone for staff to enter.

I took one last look at him and told him I loved him and that this was the best thing for him. The staff person, who was so helpful and understanding, lived on the grounds with her husband. She would assume his care and offered to give phone updates whenever I wanted.

As the days passed, I called once every week or so. The first few days, Orange Boy didn't eat, which was to be expected. She or her husband bought roasted chicken and placed it upstairs in the loft.

Orange Boy gradually returned to his old self. In time, he began coming down from the loft and was eating on a regular basis. About a month or so after his arrival, the team decided it was appropriate for him to come out and have free roam.

Now he was free—amongst all the other "residents"—hunting in the woods, residing in nice heated barns during the winter. The staff person, Annette, saw him often, walking and stalking, once again the image of the lord of the manor.

He remained in my mind's eye, and many months later, his appearances became less frequent. My last communication with

Annette was a mutual goodbye to him. As with anything living, there comes a time to leave.

All the things I wanted for Orange Boy now resided with him permanently. He was forever protected and safe, well-fortified, indestructible—and eternally my tough, indomitable, trusting friend. Now, a brave man.

Reflections on Survival

When I hear the word survival, I immediately visualize an image of strength. This applies to both animals and humans. Situations and challenges can threaten one's survival or way of life.

The responsibilities of being someone's keeper place a claim on us. As such, we strive to ensure the living or survival of others. Humans, in many instances, make choices and decisions to live. They must fuel an entire reserve of perseverance in seeking shelter from a storm. That very storm can present itself as a danger to us—physically and emotionally.

Animals, on the other hand, have emotions and feelings, but they also live by their instincts to make choices.

The concept of survival takes on greater importance in a troubled, uncertain world. Certainly, this applies to Orange Boy's life as he knew it. Living feral was an ever-changing environment thrust upon him. Choices for food, shelter, and safety required resourcefulness and adaptability.

I always viewed Orange Boy as formidable and keenly intelligent, and his outward demeanor was confident—"walking the walk," as the saying goes. Survival of his species came instinctively when fighting other cats for procreation and territorial ownership. Disputes never arose from harsh words, danger, or dislike—things that would have no place or bearing in his lifestyle.

So, what can we learn or embrace from Orange Boy's existence?

Myself—like him—despite all obstacles, emerged as victorious. Victorious over what? We learn from him to adapt ourselves, not just our environment, to navigate our way in our respective societies. To stand down to our fears, to emerge stronger, and not to give up—just as he didn't.

When he was wounded from an altercation, he was fearless in his instinct to save his strength, place some measure of trust in me, and never give up.

Survival is high stakes. Period. The rewards, however, are such that the victors are the indomitable human and animal spirits. How fortunate for me to experience the exchange of his spirit and mine.

I am proud of those who have risen like a phoenix from an uncompromising, make-or-break situation. I felt that Orange Boy instructed me—by action—on how to survive all of life's struggles. He showed no selfishness, no unethical behavior such as revenge.

Instead, the driving force of survival allowed us to come together, as well as go our separate ways. Orange Boy possessed a shining spirit that he shared with me—and most precious of all, a loving soul.

Broken Wing

"Love on the Rocks" (or ice)

Love comes to both humans and animals, presenting itself under many guises. It appears to transverse all species. Love is a force that establishes a connection between living beings. It bears no prejudice or pre-required demands. Often, it appears unexpectedly—perhaps by accident or coincidence. I would be safe in saying it arises out of primal need.

The connection that is born of it is not solely romantic; it can be a friendship or bonding, or a salient mother-and-child union. So, the saga and friendship with Broken Wing begins with this backdrop.

My home along the Hudson River proved to be a gateway for a proliferation of waterfowl, as well as an invitation to engage in their lives. The basin area adjoining my house served as a "home base," if you will, for swans, bald eagles (a rare treat), and groups of Canada Geese.

Some were either inquisitive or careless, inasmuch as they discovered an opening or break in the chain-link fencing surrounding the basin and—much to my surprise—I would find a goose wandering around the neighborhood, surveying the streets and yards. This always preceded a somewhat comical scene of my neighbors and me trying to corral them back toward the open area by the docks.

The herculean effort resembled trying to herd a bunch of cats—and of course, it always took place in the winter, when we had to surmount the piles of snow!

During the winter months, particularly the most intense, the water area became laden with ice, as there wasn't much expanse for it to spread. The geese migrated to nearby parks directly on the Hudson.

I had come to assume what I called "assisted feeding," easily done by tossing wild bird seed over the fence. The birds came together to grab the food without too much combativeness.

In my previous account of the "escapee" birds, one goose executed his or her getaway, only to be guided back to the water by me. During this rescue, I noticed there was an unnatural posturing of his/her wing. It appeared to be "angel wing," which is a syndrome in geese and ducks. The last joint of the wing is twisted and pointed outward laterally, rather than lying against the body.

Simply stated, this permanent disability prevents flying. A fellow rehabilitator came by at my request to assess his impediment, and she agreed. I might add that the gender of this bird was unknown, so allowing for some poetic license, I referred to my friend as a male. He was named Broken Wing, aka Handsome Boy (one of my many, I might add).

In addition to feeding at my house, I visited a park across from me and fed the geese. Much to my dismay, I discovered another bird with a damaged wing—much more pronounced than Broken Wing's. I was able to incorporate the assistance of another licensed rehabilitator volunteer friend to relocate the bird.

A veterinarian I worked with—who treats wildlife—consented to look at him. We were successful in directing him into a carrier with as little stress as possible. The veterinarian was able to perform surgery on the wing, but he would never fly.

She serves as the veterinarian for a local state park museum and zoo, which accepted the bird there, and he adjusted to his new surroundings in a short time.

In the meantime, I became particularly concerned that the onset of winter was a signal for the geese to migrate elsewhere. I always observed Broken Wing mingling with the others, but frankly, I never saw him pair up. As winter ensued, the basin was increasingly icing over, leaving smaller and smaller pockets of open water to swim in. Most, if not all, of the geese left—but he remained alone.

Survival came into play, and I needed a plan for, literally, his life.

At night, I could see him curled up on the ice in the extreme cold. It now occurred to me that he was totally alone, without any mate or companion. During the day, he displayed—at times—signs of grief disturbingly human. He would hang his head and seemed confused.

He needed food urgently and continuously, so every day I supplied him with corn pellets several times a day. I had really bonded with this wonderful creature and always called him by name. I would like to think that, in a small way, he had imprinted on me—although I'm sure the food was the motivating response.

I can only speak for myself when I say that I have experienced some magical, perhaps unexplainable, moments with many species. This is when my relationship became a little miracle—one I was blessed to witness.

So, the winter continued on, and Broken Wing, in spite of his compromising circumstances, was faring well. His solitary life tugged at my heart, however, as I gazed at him sitting on the ice, devoid of any companionship. Fate had isolated him with the absence of whatever partner he once had.

We were now in the month of February as I continued to care for him. On one particular day, I heard really loud honking from him. It was incessant, and I saw him standing on the ice, looking toward the entrance of the basin. The entrance was transversed by an overhead bridge that crossed over to another park.

Much to my surprise, his honking was almost rhythmic as it was answered by another bird honking from an unknown place. This exchange was like an intimate song of deep expression. I looked toward the bridge and, unbelievably, there was a goose making its way across the ice toward Broken Wing. He or she stepped from ice to open pockets of water. With each step, the bird continued honking to reply to Broken Wing.

They came together at my house, and I witnessed this deeply spiritual and loving union of these geese. Perhaps they became a male/female pair—or some gender pair—but no matter, they were co-joined. The beauty and serendipity of this event live with me to this day.

The date they bonded was February 14—Valentine's Day. Believe me, you can't make this stuff up.

Broken Wing and his companion were together from that moment on. I continued feeding them, and the last time I saw them was right before Hurricane Sandy. They had both survived Hurricane Irene the year before, but I was so apprehensive about Sandy. Many of the homes, including mine, were destroyed entirely by the storm. I had been displaced and stayed with family and friends.

The community was closed due to significant damage and losses. I no longer had access to the park and my home, which was condemned. Every morning on my way to work, I came back to the other park that was part of the bridge. I kept the corn feed in my car and fed the geese. From the bridge, I could see some geese swimming where my house once was, but I couldn't reach them.

I fervently hoped that they would come to the other park, but they didn't. Two months went by, and we were again revisiting winter. In the dark hours of the morning, I prayed to see Broken Wing and his companion.

That was not to be, as I realized they were gone. My last prayer was that they found a new home base and continued a life with each other.

Reflections on Connection

In terms of science and study, we'll never know for sure what a human is feeling—any more than we can for an animal. The point is that science has validated that they do feel!

Broken Wing came to be lost, broken, and alone. Yet through an immediate, unquestioning connection with his new partner, he showed love and a deep bonding. He found refuge without any judgment or reservation. The connection was intuitive and provided him safety.

There is an interchangeable concept here: humans are animals. Animals feel a full range of emotions, including joy, happiness, rage, anger, and love. Unlike humans, however, they express emotions through actions only.

Animal connection—such as species that mate for life—is predicated on basic terms and needs. For example, it allows for both parents to care for their young. They share the workload, guard their territory, and provide safety for each other.

It is worth noting that animals give us lessons on how to live. Their needs and values are not always what we need, but their needs and values are honest and genuine. They teach us to be compassionate and to understand the feelings of others.

Animals' lessons are the footprints we need to walk in. Looking beyond our own needs should be a guiding light. The common thread of all animals should become ours. The purity of spirit gives birth to connection.

All species have an unconditional will to love and live. They touch us and rescue us—not with words, but with senses we have never acquired. The true connection of animals is their ability to not judge human beings unkindly. The bond between human and animal is not a mere coincidence, but a deep connection from the beginning of creation.

Emulate Broken Wing when you encounter someone. Don't rely on excuses, judgment, and other devices to avoid connection with other living creatures. Open your arms and heart, and love freely. Accept love without reservation, and revel in the rewards of connection.

Open your mind—and make each and every day, Valentine's Day!

Part Four: Special Needs

Noah

"Everything is Beautiful"

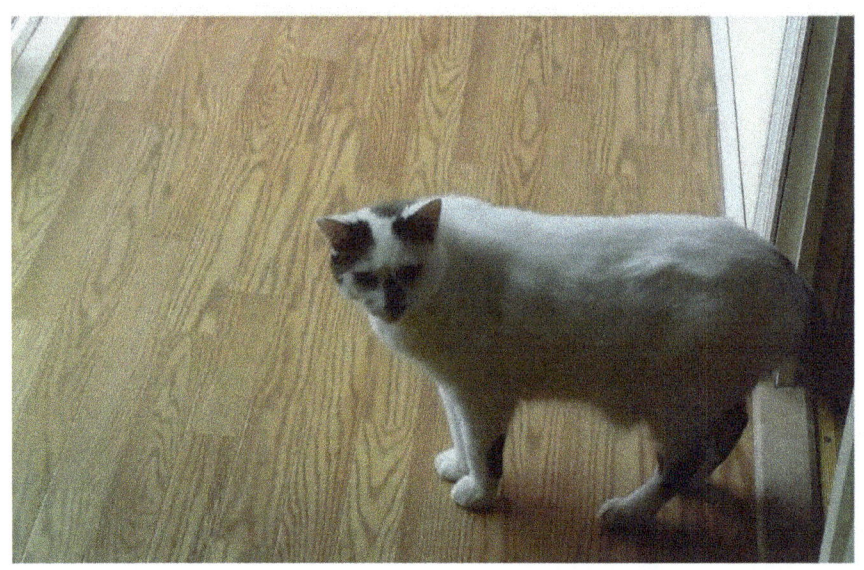

Around 2009, I was dealing with the recession like all of us, and to make it worse, I was between jobs. I decided to keep a promise I had made to myself while I had the time. So, another anonymous adoption adventure began with planning to attend a week-long conference on "Animal Sanctuaries" at Best Friends Animal Sanctuary in Utah.

One of the highlights of the trip was volunteering and interacting with any animal of interest. One of their programs allowed an overnight stay of either a pig, cat, or dog in your room, and of course, I had a variety of roommates. When you weren't in the conference, you could work with animals in their resident building. I walked with some senior dogs and chose to spend my time with senior/special needs cats.

A few of the cats that piqued my interest were already spoken for, so sadly, I left at the end of the week requesting they contact me if another cat became available.

About a week later, I was notified that a 10-year-old male cat who was blind was available. Only one problem—how did I pick him up from Utah? As it turned out, a staff member was flying into New York on shelter business and would be landing at Newark with the cat. There was no expense for the flight, just pickup at Newark Airport.

Based on his picture, I had a pretty good idea of what he looked like, but when I met him, he was absolutely disarming. He was all white with splatters of black on his feet, ears, and nose. He was a chunky boy, and I thought he resembled a Holstein cow that was all mine in miniature. My little cow was given the name Noah.

His history was interesting, as he was found living on the periphery of a feral colony. He didn't engage with the others, remaining aloof while fending for himself. His blindness certainly proved to be an impediment to food, safety, and inclusion, but apparently, he triumphed.

For the first two weeks, he was in a separate room from the other cats. I had created a "small cave" for him with blankets and an open cage, which provided some security and safety for him.

When he joined the group, he navigated around slowly and carefully but greeted each of his companions with a nose bump. It was remarkable to me that there were no skirmishes—ever. I think the others sensed his blindness and allowed him his space. Noah, on the other hand, was not bashful about laying on top of tiny Brook or saddling up to whoever was occupying a basket.

In the three years he was with me, he had blossomed into a "mushy" couch potato who loved being petted and brushed. I believe his built-in GPS enabled him to follow me, and whenever I stood over him and made a clucking or clicking noise, he would fall down and lay on his side for attention. My old man resembled the goats that fall over when stared at.

By this time, at 13, Noah spent most of his time sleeping. He was diagnosed with congestive heart failure, which ultimately took him.

What a rare treasure I found in the gorgeous canyons of Utah. He became confident, and his blindness led me to believe in miracles.

Reflections on Other-Abled

It would seem enough when life deals us not one, but far too many surprises. Sometimes enough is not enough, and our creativity, patience, and faith must step in.

People and animals who are subject to several disabilities often meet their challenges with the will and resourcefulness of compensation.

When I met Noah, I immediately recognized that he was not disabled. In my mind, labeling him as such was condescending or patronizing. He displayed a resilience and fearlessness accorded to those who are simply different.

Noah began life as feral, alone and living in the loneliness without eyesight. A perfect analogy would be a blind person sitting on the sidewalk, homeless and seeking help from people walking by.

Both are guided to not only survive but develop empowerment. They discover environments that serve as refuge and guarantee safety. Their inner spirit lights their way and strengthens their resolve and will to live.

Noah was not provided inclusivity, safety, or protection. Survival was the determining factor. When he was adopted, he began living as he was gifted love and attention. He unearthed intuitive trust.

Fear of human contact and a dark world were replaced with connection and bonding. A vision unrelated to his blindness was born of this.

You see, Noah was indeed rescued from a world devoid of everything, except survival. The love he received and gave freed him from the bondage of being lost and forgotten.

He may have had no vision, but he saw more clearly than he ever had.

Everything regarded or viewed as a disability was transformed into strengths and beauty.

With both animals and humans, be generous in providing support. Give freely of emotional and spiritual love. Every "Noah" you meet is beautiful. Let them experience your beauty.

Their existence is nothing short of a miracle.

They are not handicapped, not flawed, not deficient. They are other-abled!

Jeremy

"Gird Your Loins"

As many people discover, a trip to an animal shelter warrants preparation. Even though you may have a specific breed or gender in mind, never lose sight of the diversity of behavior, personalities, and responsiveness you will encounter. The emotional landscape of the cats and dogs could be fear, aggression, retreat, or affection.

What if you find that a pet you select demonstrates all of the aforementioned? I suggest, at this juncture, to arm yourself with the biblical armor of "gird your loins." In other words, I myself was excited about adopting a cat but soon found out that this may be a bumpy ride. So, this is the perfect segue to introduce Jeremy and his story!

I think I was drawn to Jeremy at hello. He appeared to be the usual tabby in coat design and somewhat "worn" looking. The staff person said his name was Theremy, which in translation means "victorious" and the spirit of God. What a strange name, I thought, and felt we could do better. The saying goes, "You say tomato, I say tomato." By virtue of that, he became Jeremy.

Jeremy came home with me and, as expected, was anxious and unapproachable. There was no indication that he would strike out, but that is precisely what he did when I simply walked by him. A few scratches later on my legs, he backed into a corner and crouched in silence with a dark look across his face. I knew right then that hisses were not soon to be kisses.

I discovered quickly that his mouth and teeth were causing him discomfort. The vet examined him and felt that he was an older cat and that the teeth were significantly decayed. A full-mouth extraction was in order, and I hoped that this would explain his behavior. Jeremy recovered well, but his disposition failed to improve. The only choice I had was to persevere and gain his trust amidst a flurry of scratches and bloodletting once or more a day. Thankfully, I suffered no bites— as he was toothless.

I became more and more attached to Jeremy, although I was a glutton for punishment. There was a softer side to him, which I recognized in his facial expression. He was finding a comfort zone— however small it was—and began to grant me permission to pet him gently and quickly, I might add. He was definitely guarding himself and kept in check the desire to be disagreeable more often my fellow technicians and veterinarians where I worked all knew Jeremy. This was in part due to the preparation and theatrics created by him when he came in for bloodwork. Usually, a docile, angry cat can be easily restrained by one tech—or two, at least. Oh no, not Jeremy. Here we have a 7 to 8 lb. wiry thin cat causing pandemonium, forcing the vet to come down the hallway exclaiming, "All right, team—time for battle! Gird your loins!"

I am smiling already as I visually recall this scene. In retrospect, we were not behaving abusively toward Jeremy, but finding humor in this cat needing two technicians holding him by the back legs while he was howling, hissing, and squirming his body with all his might. I would be restraining his front legs while someone else was tapping his forehead to distract him. The tapping is an effective trick with most cats; however, the technician doing it had a tiny plastic baseball bat on his keychain that he tapped on Jeremy. Needless to say, it was not a huge success—but we all succumbed to laughter.

Jeremy made it clear that he had an abundance of comments to make. We put him in a comfortable cage to relax until we were ready to go home. Every time someone came near the cage—or even walked by—he pounced on the door and spit! Yes, he did spit—not saliva, just the noise to express his disdain for his undignified treatment.

This was the gift that I saw more and more frequently in Jeremy. He had the uncanny ability to be aggressive, yet possessed this desperate longing to belong. No one was afraid of him, but instead loved him. He could pass off a great deal of charm when he was so inclined.

Jeremy resided at home with my five other cats. As I expected, my band of cats were relatively unimpressed with his arrival. An interesting dynamic occurred as to the balance between all of them. I was fully prepared to see Jeremy climb to the top of the hierarchy ladder, but instead he retreated to his isolated space. Occasionally, he would hiss at the others, but even that was infrequent. The other guys seemed to either honor his space or protect themselves from harm's way. In any event, the coexistence was quickly laid out in broad terms. A peaceful environment was sustained.

When I describe Jeremy, another term comes into play: "like quicksilver," which describes almost all cats in their ability to bite, scratch, and do so in an extremely fine-tuned, orchestrated manner when threatened. I, for one, can attest to a cat bite being a hundred times worse than a dog bite any day.

Jeremy did like to sleep at the foot of the bed, while the other cats laid claim to parts of the bed away from him. He was very protective of that space and would hiss if anyone came too close—including my toes, which he also enjoyed chewing.

I came to read him very well and recognized when he was interested in engaging with me. I would sit in my favorite armchair, and he would sit directly in front of me at my feet. I would tap my lap to encourage him to come up, which he did. He would crouch into a ball on my lap, allowing me to pet him. It never lasted long, and with a hissy announcement, he would ceremoniously jump off his throne.

I marveled at the dichotomy: never wanting to mingle or interact with the rest of the brood, but feeling safe enough with me—no matter how short the pleasantry.

Jeremy's age was catching up with him, approaching 16 or 17 years old. His energy level had diminished, as well as his appetite. After a barrage of tests, we discovered he had lymphoma. The diagnosis was poor, inasmuch as his immune system was markedly compromised. The best we could do was provide a regimen of Leukeran, a cancer medication to keep him comfortable. The prognosis, in and of itself, convinced me to provide hospice care at home until such time there was no more quality of life.

Jeremy, for all intents and purposes and under God's watchful eye made the decision with me. He was lying on several blankets in the waning hours. What occurred was a connection, innately and spiritually exchanged, with my other cats. They went up to him one at a time, as if they knew not to overwhelm him. They ever so gently sniffed him and lingered for perhaps a minute or so. It was the closest facsimile to viewing a human counterpart who will soon pass.

Jeremy moved on peacefully and gently, with, finally, full trust and love which he so deserved and found.

Reflections on Holy Anointing

When I remember Jeremy, there is a remnant of sadness and empathy. There is no question that I used every opportunity at my disposal to provide him with a quality life.

I can't help but wonder, though, what kind of history he carried. Was he a stray? Was he neglected in his home? Was he abused? Was he lost and couldn't find his way? Was there a psychological trigger or deficit that he brought into the world?

Jeremy was encased in a shell that was solitary and lonely, but it also provided him protection. I sensed from the beginning that he was a special needs cat. Some component of his personality was absent, yet the remainder of his character was very special.

Deep inside of him, past the fear and mistrust, was a hidden space that held his anointing. There, in that sanctuary or tabernacle, a glimmer of his desire to belong became tangible. Over the years, that light became brighter and brighter, and his shield diminished in its value.

Humans and animals are all bequeathed anointing. That gift enables a spiritual connection. In some cases, humans do not recognize this and stumble along the way without touching others. How or why remains to be seen. However, they nurture and cling to anxiety, guarding their emotions, lack of trust, and loneliness. This was a picture of Jeremy as well.

Humans should use their private shield in a different context—not to be worn as an object, but to actively shield others beside yourself. Allow yourself to ignore defenses and find common ground with others. Free yourself from loneliness and embrace humanity.

Jeremy was guided in the anointing to overcome his obstacles and challenges. The need and desire to possess love, security, and safety became his driving force. This is a prayer for you as well. Go to that space—that tabernacle, if you will—and open the door for the light to direct you. Open your heart to experience a transformational connection.

Jeremy and I were kindred spirits. Fate brought us together, and we both found the security and comfort that we alone could not sustain. His dance became my dance. We moved as one—a fluidity rarely experienced with any living thing. In the end, his pain became my pain, and so the curtains fell, with each of us pulling the cords. He did not fall victim to his deficits but instead stayed the course and retained the ultimate blessing of love and companionship.

My blessing was his choice of me!

I hope all can follow the path of openness and transparency. Listen to your inner voice. No one can hurt you. You deserve love that transforms you.

Go out and find your "Jeremy," whoever that may be. Ignore the hisses and scratches along the way, for they are only temporary signposts.

The reward is a blessing for all time.

Brook

"Ode to an Angel"

It is believed that angels come to Earth and serve as intermediaries or messengers. They act as guides, protectors, and guardians. I believe that angels not only take on human form but appear in animal form as well. I also believe that once in a lifetime, a non-human angel comes to live when Heaven and Earth overlap. This special place and spirit unite humans and animals in a way that is supernatural.

We are about to meet Brook—my unexpected yet predestined guide and teacher. I was blessed with an all-time love, though I didn't know it at the time.

It was a normal day about 15 years ago when my staff and I made a trip to the NYC Animal Control facilities, with whom we worked. We specifically made contact to identify dogs and cats who were adoptable and could find permanent homes through us.

We arrived that day at the Brooklyn Center and began conversing with their staff. I was standing at the front desk when I noticed a young man—perhaps a construction worker, judging by his appearance—carrying a closed box. I was close enough to hear his conversation with someone at the desk, explaining how he had rescued a young cat.

He had been working at a building site when he saw a group of young kids noisily standing in a circle around what appeared to be a kitten or older cat. Indeed, it was a cat—being taunted and kicked relentlessly by the kids. The young man chased them away and picked up the cat, which he now had with him at the desk.

Since I knew the staff there, I asked what they planned to do and asked them to inform me. I didn't know if euthanasia was in order just yet, but I did know we would take her back to our shelter. I spoke to the vet, who assessed her trauma as a fractured femur and pelvis. He couldn't guarantee that her mobility would be intact, but he recommended cage rest for an extended period and suggested we explore further diagnostics with our shelter vets.

My staff and I boarded the van, and I sat in the passenger seat holding the cat in a towel. I somehow sensed an extremely deep connection with her and instinctively recognized the introduction to each other as something that transcended the laws of nature. I picked up this frail, diminutive cat and placed her against me, and without any hesitation or fear, she placed her front paws over my shoulders and began to knead.

One of the staff in the back seat marked this moment with a single sentence:

"If this isn't rescue, I don't know what is!"

Our bond became cemented then and there.

This cat was not a kitten, but estimated to be about two years of age. She was named Brook, since she was found in Brooklyn. It seemed original at the time, as she appeared to be this little waif, weighing in at about seven pounds or so.

Brook was so unique that you couldn't help but laugh. She was polydactyl (six-toed), which made it look like she was wearing mittens. Her face slightly resembled an Ewok, but her eyes were captivating. They were larger than life—absolutely global. It seemed that her eyes were open as wide as possible, and her gaze looked like a pool or a lake. The softness of her face was beckoning—to be seen, to be held, to be spoken to. All the things you find in an infant, for example.

This was my first glimpse into her mesmeric charm as well as her helplessness.

Brook remained crated for several weeks with very few adverse symptoms. Initially, she displayed this involuntary back leg movement or undulation, which eventually dissipated. Brook became a resident in my office, along with her roommate, Porter, who we will meet further on.

Her gait was one of her most unusual deficits. Her left leg extended outward from her body, and she seemed to slide rather than walk. Her nickname became—and always remained—"Slip and Slide."

There was little we knew about her physiologically, other than the trauma from her abuse. It was evident there was some neurological damage, considering her balance issues and impaired sight in one eye. I guarded her carefully and feared that "the other shoe" would ultimately drop.

That first drop came months later.

Brook began circling again and displayed her involuntary gait. She was dehydrated and neither drank nor ate. I literally fed her with a baby spoon, holding her wrapped in a towel—and she wore most of the food. Force feeding was imperative as her weight was dropping.

Brook was seen by a board-certified neurologist who recommended a CAT scan to better understand her decline. Putting her under anesthesia was a challenge in and of itself, but of course, it was necessary.

The results of her CAT scan were shocking, in that the nature of this injury was quite rare. The scan showed trauma to her brain. On one side, the vet felt this could have been caused by the abuse or possibly being hit by a car. The left side of her brain was devoid of brain matter—anything that had been injured became necrotic and died.

When the scan was done, they began removing her from anesthesia, extubating her, and waiting for her to "pink up." Instead, she suffered a spontaneous pneumothorax (collapsed lung) and had to be resuscitated by the team.

In the end, she proved herself not a victim, but a survivor.

Brook consistently had discrepancies in her bloodwork lab results. She had kidney issues, but again, an anomaly with her sodium and potassium levels. What was high for a normal cat was normal for Brook, and so I religiously administered fluids once a day, every day.

Over the years, I was mystified by the nature of her infant-like behavior and needs. She was a spirit reborn—perhaps saved. Here she was, this little infant from within, sharing her innocence and warmth. I believe that no matter how vulnerable and helpless she appeared, she was uncorrupted. She was pure and honest in her need for me, just as I was in my need for her.

Here is an example of her frailty and her need to be complete:

Before her ambulation became compromised, she easily jumped on and off the bed. I would be sleeping, lying on my left side. She would saddle up to me and, I expect, evaluate this big mountain—my

93

back. She decided the best approach was climbing, so she stroked my back first with her right, then her left leg—much akin to rock climbing, except I was the rock.

She was able to drag herself up to the top of Everest, but would begin to slide down the other side, losing her grip. I would hold her and turn over onto my back. It was here that my heart melted into a reservoir of gratitude and awe—of being a recipient of her primal love. I would take her paw and cup it into the palm of my hand, and she, ever so deliberately and lovingly, took hold of one index finger of mine. I thought, This is what a baby does!

Brook exacted this routine every night until illness overtook her.

Brook was entering her 13th or 14th year when her back legs were ostensibly weakening and losing support. She could no longer jump from the floor to the mattress. I removed the box spring and lowered the mattress considerably. As time went on, she was able to slide over the edge to the floor but still couldn't get up. She was also having difficulty eating. Her teeth had deteriorated, as she could never sustain herself under anesthesia.

So, now Nightingale Watch would be her comfort.

I gave her the dignity to walk, but when it overtook her, I carried her around like an infant. I assisted her with eating, but she couldn't chew as well. Finally, her weight had plummeted to 3 to 4 lbs.

The time had now arrived to determine whether there remained any quality to her life. I think she looked to me the same way I looked at her.

That morning, she kept sitting in the bedroom doorway—with, oh, those big eyes—almost plaintive, yet prayerful.

When we arrived at the clinic for the euthanasia, Brook was simply Brook. She was not fearful, not afraid—just reliant on me for all things good. Once again, for the last time, she performed another miracle as a gift for me.

As you may know, before euthanasia, the animal is administered a sedative and becomes unaware. I continued to hold her in a blanket as she looked at me with those eyes. She didn't resist in pain but instead was completely calm. In all my years of these moments, I have never been blessed with such a message of gratitude and readiness to go home.

She ever so gently yawned—two times—with little effort. Wide-eyed wonder, trust in me, rewarding me with her love and that of God.

My peaceful, beautiful girl was literally walking the straight and narrow. No turns. No tumbles. Directly en route to her home.

Brook lives on. She is not gone. Her physicality challenged her, but she responded bravely. She taught me the simplest, yet irrefutable truths: always keep your childlike ways alive. Widen your eyes and gaze at life with wonder.

Remember, a few "slip and slides" are nothing. You are strong. Bask in these moments—when someone holds your fingers or hand, gives you a blanket of love with a hug, and carries you when things get tough.

Reflections on Pureness of Heart

All animal lovers share the same passions—joy, disappointments, and yes, even pain. Animals, in the blink of an eye, run off with your heart, yet you never feel robbed. In the end, however, they splinter our hearts into a million pieces when they die.

I believe our pets—my pet, Brook—live on. She is only deceased in her physical being. She lives on—and why?

Brook came into this world as an angel incarnate. She embodied love, selflessness, unquestioning trust, and she was assigned a mission. Brook was not only innocent, but she was also pure in heart. She didn't create this or find this—no—she served as a vessel to preserve and share this virtue.

Being pure in heart is one and the same as innocence. Brook was also meek. She never forced herself on the other cats in the household. She introduced herself every day with a nuzzle, but if she was rebuffed, she stepped back and turned that "proverbial cheek." She was a shining example of a Beatitude: "Blessed are the pure of heart, for they shall see God."

It doesn't matter your belief in a God or specific religion—being pure of heart is a common thread that elevates our humanity and ties us all together as one.

Brook had the eyes and heart of a child. She was blessed, and she generously gifted us with her blessing. She was able to lay claim to a poignant, hungry, and thirsty piece of us that lay anonymous.

We need to open our hearts to others. Like Brook, continue to seek love in spite of your meekness. Recognize your vulnerabilities and move forward above them. Grab onto someone's hand and trust them. Keep your eyes open to everything, and listen to your heart's subtle whispers and murmurs—those that rustle like an angel's wings and carry you on this journey called life.

Emulate Brook: meek, but open; hurt, but still possessing wide-eyed wonder; vulnerable, but fearless; filled with love and guided by a brilliant light which you share with others like a warm blanket.

Nightingale Watch

Reflections on Hospice and Palliative Care
" A Kiss Goodnight for Your Journey"

The nightingale's song is sad, plaintive, yet brilliant. The song is filled with trills, roulades, whistles, and gurgles. Many years ago, during the spring and summer months, I discovered this mysterious, musical treasure punctuating the dark night. In the blackness and stillness of the night, I was awakened—or rather, gently prodded—to sit up and press my ear to the window screen. Perhaps my first instinct was to convince myself it was a dream, for the sounds were evocative of a place and things I had never visited before.

The nightingale was a voice in the night, sent to provide comfort during dark hours. Groups of nightingales are termed a "watch", though collectively trilling in a singular voice of nature that is exquisite in its purity. Their lullaby awakened a force so spiritual in me that I longed to share my existence with other creatures in providing hospice care. That evening, I was guided by a force greater than me.

The mission, in turn, blossomed into a ministry. I was enveloped in a calm and soothing companionship. The suspension of all sound, other than the songs, freed me from fear of the unfriendly night.

This was communication—a sing-song salutation in perfect synchrony to fly away with them in heart and soul. This first encounter forever steeped my soul with comfort, compassion, and hope. It was here that my hospice care took shape and name. Even in sadness, pain, and ultimate transition, a joyous symphony serenades each soul and carries them through the night to light and love.

Those of us who love all animals take on the role of hospice caretaker. We take care of our pets and support them to the very end. Some, on rare occasions, leave this place by the hand of God. We assume the responsibility and privilege of ending suffering and pain. The mutual discourse between us tells us that quality of life no longer exists. With the exception of one, all 23 of my pets left with me by their side.

For every departure, there is an arrival. My participation in the journey has gifted me with an intimacy bequeathed to only a few. If only for a fleeting moment, your eyes connect, and two souls come together. This perfect, pure communion is an elevation to a mystical exchange of trust and gratitude. I believe this to be a "visitation" from a power greater than ours.

My memories of my animals, for which I prayed and held in my arms, remain vivid. Their supplicant expression was an exchange of a blessing. It was then that my breath was taken away, for their soul went through mine. I have been, and remain, humbled by caring for my pets and patients. In the end, my parting gift was a kiss goodnight for a safe journey home.

Allow me to share the chronicles of Nightingale Watch.

Vignettes of Love

I sit and sometimes ponder the universal question: "Where has all the time gone?" If you're still here with many years behind you, consider yourself fortunate and blessed. I think about quantity versus quality. Getting old is actually a gift, but you may not recognize it as one, as you get caught up in your poor quality of life—or lack of it, for that matter. Quality of life is not always a gift; you must contribute. When stillness overcomes you, thoughts bounce around, seeking an escape from your guarded mind. Once we shake out the cobwebs in the crevices of our heart, we see all moments: joys, events, successes, anger, grief, etc. Assessing this internal inventory takes courage. A door is open to you, with a compass to navigate your travel, and along the way, you garner ownership of compassion, guardianship, and reverence. In turn, you are redeemed.

So, many years ago, the door was open to me. Although I felt connected to animals, I was not fully aware of the responsibility and obligation of such a commitment. It was a warm summer night that I still remember clearly to this day. I was leaving a friend's house when, outside in the dark, I heard a noise—a plaintive whisper of a cry coming from the shrubs. I grabbed a flashlight from my car and, looking toward the plants, I was stunned to find a tiny kitten, at least

2–3 months old. I went back inside, grabbed a towel, and returned to wrap up the kitten. When I got home, I arranged a bed for her in the bathroom so she would be separated from my other cats. This little creature was helpless, perhaps abandoned by her mother, but nonetheless, she was being afforded one last chance to live. At this time, I did not possess a great deal of experience or knowledge concerning animals. I suppose I was directed by instinctive Good Samaritan teachings.

Her fur was matted with sections missing. She had small wounds and what appeared to be maggots. Her nostrils and eyes were covered with dried mucus. I gently combed her out and cleared up all the areas. I tried to hand-feed her, but to no avail. This entire situation was gut-wrenching, as there were few and far-between emergency hospitals, so I sat with her wrapped in a blanket and held her against my chest most of the night. Towards morning, she began to demonstrate some neurological issues, which unbeknownst to me, were seizures. She simply and quietly passed away that day, and in doing so, breathed a message to me from her soul—a thank you for saving her.

That moment marked the inception of Nightingale Watch, as a state of mind. This little kitten's death gave way to the birth of my mission in life. She was safely home, and I initiated my life's work with one simple gesture: I kissed her on her forehead with a blessing and a prayer. From that day forward, I have shared this sacrament with every single animal in my home or elsewhere.

I invite you to meet and bless all that follow in the collective gallery of vignettes. All have completed their visit on Earth, and all were loved. Most especially, I remember the kitten with tears of gratitude, inasmuch as I was permitted to give her a few precious hours to hold her, protect her, and free her. She was not alone. She was revered and rescued, if only for a short while. If only for a short time, she was loved.

She was the beginning of a love story for all time—my love story.

Lady and Sabrina

I moved to my present location when I was young, around 15 or so, if memory serves me correctly. My family had always lived in rentals in the city until this move to a house.

I was fortunate in receiving a gift so unexpected and amazing. Talk about someone who was clearly self-assured and confident. The beauty that comes through that confidence was that of a rock star. You're probably curious who this person was, but believe me, it was love at first sight. No, it wasn't a new friend or schoolmate or even a family member. It was an elegant, handsome German Shepherd. This wonderful creature took my breath away because of her beauty, but especially because she was my very first pet. I named her Lady and was indebted to my dad, who favored Shepherds and rescued her from a shelter. She was about 2–3 years old and had been in the shelter for quite a while.

Lady had very sad eyes—not inviting, but lifeless, as though the spirit in her had simply evaporated. She allowed me to sit next to her when we met, but she was wary and became rigid in her stance when I got too close. The first night she shared my bedroom proved to be heartbreaking. I found her under my bed in the morning, with her face literally under the bed and only her hind end protruding outward.

Gently, I was able to coax her to come out, but there were these frightened eyes and concern in her eyebrows.

Lady was welcomed into our family by everyone, but her bond with me strengthened by the day. She became more relaxed. There evolved an interchange of affection, both physically and verbally. Gradually, she not only responded to touch and petting and hearing her name, but she sought it out. As time went on, it seemed that Lady never went back to her fear and insecurity. Instead, she blossomed and exhibited positive affirmation of simple pleasures such as toys, running in the yard, and laying on her own bed. In return for these simple pleasures, she gave me her all and never failed to display her gratitude for her new life. Life was beyond good for she and I. I reveled in this privilege of her "owning" me as I did her.

Ultimately, Lady became quite old and debilitated by severe arthritis, hip dysplasia, and lack of vision. When she passed, I was brokenhearted. I was naïve and ill-equipped for this part of loving an animal, but little did I know what lay ahead. My time with Lady was a gift—a pathway to so many, many amazing other animals that would make me who I am. Thank you, Lady, for lessons well taught.

It didn't take very long for God's hand to place me in His providence. Doors began to open, allowing me to enter planned introductions.

It was at this time in my journey that another animal was to come into my life. My friend lived in a heavily populated apartment complex with lots of children. Apparently, there was a stray near her apartment who appeared to be quite young and wandering the complex. She was constantly intervening with the kids who were tormenting the dog by throwing sticks and rocks. The dog needed some help and protection, so, who did she approach? You guessed it— me! I wasn't fooling anyone, especially not myself, that my name was all over the rescue. My friend brought her over, and my reaction was, "Be still my heart." She was probably about 1–1.5 years old at best. I suppose by now you already realize what she looked like. Yes, she was a breathtaking black and tan German Shepherd.

This gentle creature, a baby in my mind, seemed almost relieved to be saved from her abusers. Her eyes, like all Shepherds, were animated yet calm. She showed no hostility or fear; rather, she was open to engagement and curious. This little girl became Sabrina, and she kept Lady's presence ever present in the commonality of their personalities. The difference in them was also pronounced. Sabrina bonded very quickly to me, and it was strong. She would nudge me, paw, and mouth me—but solely me. She was much more guarded with other family members and distinctly aloof with people outside of us. During her life, one of her favorite treats was riding in the car. She was very comical because, at 60–70 lbs., she liked to sit side by side, particularly in my lap. If she got loose from the yard, all I had to do was shout, "Let's go for a car ride," and she would come running.

Sabrina, like Lady, had a good life for many years. She lived within a family of two other dogs and five cats. She conjured up an image of royalty overseeing her dominion, and all was good. She passed away from kidney failure, and in my grief over her, I thought lovingly of Lady. There was a hole in my heart, but only for a short time because it became filled with all the joy, happiness, and companionship they both gave me. As Shepherds, they taught me how to protect, guide, and watch over others as they did me.

Samantha, Sasha and BB (Baby Boy)

Although I love all animals of every size, shape, and breed, I acknowledge a special place in my heart for German Shepherds. Their intelligence and handsome appearance steal my heart away every time. Lest we forget cats, a breed much beloved is the Siamese. As shocking as it might seem, I had not one but three chocolate seal points living together with me. All of them were rescued from a shelter, given up by owners for reasons I cannot fathom.

Samantha and Sasha were already seniors, and Baby Boy was about 1 to 2 years old. It didn't seem strange to me at the time to adopt three Siamese, although I did not have any particular interest or desire to visit Thailand. I remember how striking they were with the chocolate points and stunning blue eyes. Baby Boy had the additional signature of being cross-eyed. His ears were so long and pointy that it was hard to imagine him growing into them. They did, however, give him an intelligent expression.

The trait I found most endearing was their desire to chat and chat some more. A quiet cat they were not. Some people are put off by their vocalization, which sounds very much like an infant crying. They certainly get your attention. By the way, they don't quit until they get what they want.

The three of them got along famously. They cuddled with each other and with me. Sasha seemed to favor a bit more personal space, but at any given time, they were demanding attention from me. All three were velcro cats, following me wherever I went, and if it seemed obvious to them, they screamed for my worship and adoration.

My little "Siams" were sociable to the ninth degree. They equally bonded with me and wanted me as their best friend. They truly amazed me with their beauty, affection, intelligence, and high energy. No day was complete without a noisy conversation.

I was drawn to them by a force directing me to save and fulfill their lives. I was able to provide them with love and care that Sam and Sasha so deserved in their few remaining years. BB was my blue-eyed handsome boy for 15 years. He, as well as the girls, was a shining light in an otherwise predictable, mediocre life.

As the saying goes, "best friends forever."

Sassy

Fate dictates whether you are in the right place at the right time—or not. At the time, I wasn't sure which applied to me. I look back now and unequivocally know it was all right! It was when I found Sassy.

Sassy was the first cat I ever owned as an adult. She was probably about two years old and quite striking with her black and white markings. She appeared unexpectedly, living on the perimeter of the school grounds where I was employed. It was fall, and the staff and I were entertained by her frolicking carelessly, playing amongst piles of leaves. We started to leave food for her and noticed that she was somewhat rotund and less energetic. I decided to bring her into the building and set up housekeeping in a spare room. It occurred to me that she might be pregnant, but after several weeks, there were no labor pains, less abdominal swelling, and increased energy. The presumptive diagnosis by the veterinarian was likely a false pregnancy.

In any event, she couldn't continue living in the building, so she came home with me. There were three other cats at home, and soon, we found the most fitting name for her in short order. Sassy was formidable in the most fitting way with her new companions. She was first at the food bowl, first on a cat bed, and first in the window— simply through physical interference. She could be very sweet and docile with them as well as with me, but only to a point. If she became irritated, Sassy became "sassy."

There emerged a great deal of harmony in the household. Sassy wore this invisible mantle as head cat or matriarch. Her gentleness was uniform, her messaging clear, and her confidence unrestrained.

Sassy remembered all of her acrobatics from the outdoors. She was always leaping onto window sills or climbing on tables to propel herself in one leap to the top of the kitchen cabinets. She loved to tease—or at times antagonize—another cat when hidden under the couch by swiping at them with her paw as they walked by. Usually, they were just startled, but at times, a brawl would begin, lasting only a moment or so.

Her most daring feat, if not her final one, was her investigating the pipe under the kitchen sink. There was an open space around the circumference of the pipe. With it being unusually large and her being far too inquisitive, it was the perfect storm of cat drama. Somehow, when I was in another room, she managed to open the cabinet door. To this day, I still can't conceive how she squeezed into the opening and went under the floorboard. I heard these piercing cries, and to my shock, found them coming from below the pipes. Sassy certainly had a guardian angel that day, as I kept repeatedly calling her by name, and she was able to retrace her way back through the opening! Then and there, I had a clear illustration of why childproof locks need to be placed on cabinet doors.

Sassy had a wonderful life and reached her 21st year before she succumbed to kidney failure. She was the first of many "firsts." She was regal and deserving of her stature within the family. Little did I know that she would be the beloved predecessor of a long lineage of cats. The love I have for her keeps my heart and memories alive.

Jeep

It seems wherever I go, I stumble upon "hidden" treasures. It always appears that I am not seeking them out; they find me. If this sounds familiar, welcome to the mission of rescue.

Jeep was one of many creatures I have come upon, hidden under bushes. He was about three or four months old and was totally alone—no litter, no siblings, no mother. He offered no resistance when I picked him up, and although I'm sure he had not been around people, he was quite docile and calm. He was a beautiful kitten, covered with white and gold splashes of color. At that time, I was driving a Jeep vehicle, and since he was the first animal I had rescued with this car, I decided to name him Jeep (later known as the "Jeepster)".

From the very beginning, he easily acclimated to his new home, but more importantly, he related well to the dynamics of the group of other cats. In short order, he proved himself to be quite affectionate and engaging, and the response from the others was reciprocated.

He effortlessly bonded with each cat—not selective of one in particular, but equally comfortable with them all. I always felt that Jeep stepped into his role of "ambassador" instinctively. Never was there any friction, just serenity, mutual affection, and individual space for one and all.

I always remember that Jeep could be very playful, as he was the youngest of this clowder of cats. His one idiosyncrasy, which was comical, was his fascination with ladies' nails. Friends who visited, maintaining nails of some length, immediately drew Jeep to them. If they were sitting in a chair with their hands draped over the arm, Jeep never missed a beat. He would immediately go over and paw gently at their nails or brush against their fingers. An exceptional attraction to someone's nails would even elicit a few licks. What an ingenious way to render a "kitty" manicure.

Jeep found a wonderful life with all his other companions. In the midst of dogs, cats, and even birds, he spent quality time in cat beds, looking out windows, and claiming his spot on the bed with me.

All animals, in my opinion, are a gift. However, Jeep was one of the most peaceable animals I ever knew. His presence in my home, although understated, commanded harmony and goodwill.

Jeep was coming up to his tenth birthday when his departure became a reality. As in the expression, "it happened overnight," Jeep was fine one day and ill the next. He had stopped eating and crouched into a ball, huddled by the bathroom sink. He immediately went to the veterinary hospital, where it was discovered that he had cardiac issues. It was necessary to leave him under hospital care, as it was what was best for him. His time was set, and his mission complete, when I received the news that he passed away overnight.

Upon Jeep's passing, I felt great guilt for not being with him, but I was reminded that there is no calendar or clock provided to us as to when humans or animals die.

I knew with all my heart that Jeep went home completely at peace. His life was generous in what it granted to all who knew him. He filled space that was empty, healed wounds with gentleness, and created a home free from strife or disorder.

Jeep was a gentle soul who embraced me with his purity, tranquility, and peace. Thank you, Jeep, for guarding my heart and mind now and forever.

Jessie

It's amazing to me how animals enter your life more often than not when you least expect it. You encounter them as strays, lost and unfound, abused, or relinquished by people, but rarely by choice. The story of Jessie bears witness to the lackadaisical behavior of some people.

I was living in a development where there were always a cat or two exploring the area, most of them strays. One particular cat always came to my yard and surveyed the area for food. He certainly appeared healthy and not underfed by any stretch of the imagination—a big, handsome boy, easily a 10-pounder with striking tabby markings. I assumed he was feral, but not so, as he readily came to me and posed no aggression. The visitation routine went on for about two weeks or so, and I asked around my neighborhood if anyone was missing a cat. Each inquiry was a dead end, so I took him in under the supposition that he was a stray.

About this time, or even a little later, I got a knock on my door and found a young man standing there. He didn't introduce himself but said he wanted me to know he saw his girlfriend's cat at my house. I replied that I was glad there was an owner. His reply not only baffled and surprised me, but quite frankly angered me. He said they didn't like me feeding him. I asked him at that point why he or she didn't inquire earlier. I was dumbfounded when he replied that I shouldn't have taken him. You would think it perfectly natural for me to have him reclaim his cat in light of accusing me of "cat-napping." I was simply nonplussed when he informed me that they didn't want him back—he was too much trouble—and walked away. My only thought was the future care of this cat, and that was me. This was how Jessie came to be.

From the first day in his new family, Jessie took to his new home like a duck to water. He did not establish any bond with others, but rather a take-charge, aloof persona. Jessie actually was a gentle giant, a real couch potato. I think his size alone was enough to keep everyone else in their respective places.

The first years, he enjoyed companionship, attention, and an array of creature comforts. He definitely was overweight, but that never hindered him in any way. It was around that time that he showed a weight loss that was barely noticeable, except to me. He also, on occasion, would stop walking and lay down. Every so often, he exhibited a cough. All of these distinct yet unrelated markers were, in fact, related, and the sum of the parts spelled trouble.

His medical workup proved nothing less than devastating. A small growth of the tiniest size was indicative of lymphoma. He had surgery to remove it immediately, and the size of the growth proved to be a blessing. Jesse was laid up for a week or two and began chemotherapy. He responded well to the regimen; however, there was a black cloud hanging over us in that he was diagnosed with bronchitis and congestive heart failure. He stoically accepted all his treatments— administered a breathalyzer several times a day, medications, and more trips to the ER than I care to remember when fluid built up around his heart and had to be tapped.

Jesse consistently fought the good fight. I think he knew that I was doing everything I could to keep some quality in his life. All of this was more than I could handle at times. The veterinarian prepared me for the reality of the congestive heart failure. In the simplest terms possible, he wanted me to know that the probability of me finding him dead was high. In those days, how I wanted to rail at everyone and everything—scream to a higher power, the universe, the doctors, and myself over the inequity and injustice placed on Jessie.

As time went on, we forged ahead, and on this day that was to be predestined, I tried to apply the breathalyzer to Jessie, and it was the only time ever that he resisted vigorously. I told him, "Okay," and wouldn't upset him anymore. I remember looking at him on the bed before I left for work, and the look in his eyes went right through me. Was he telling me he was tired, that he wanted to be alone, that he thanked me, that he loved me? I'll never know. I came home late from work and greeted everyone, calling out to him. Perplexed at not finding him anywhere, I glanced over to the litter box in the bathroom, only to find him lying in the box. He had died on his own terms.

What I remember most about Jessie was his resiliency and his patience. If he could speak, he never uttered a complaint, never angry over the hand he was dealt, and never doubted that, in spite of all his challenges, he had a deep, intimate life with his family. His bravery inspired me to incorporate all of this into my life as well. I know that Jessie left this world with all my love to carry him.

Queenie Girl and Jenny Rebecca

Once again, I am amazed at the differences between animals and humans, but more so the commonalities. Sadly, so many animals are lost, broken, and neglected, but there again, so are people. How often do you see young people disowned or cut off from their own families due to a poor judgment call? Animals, too, are abandoned for reasons unclear to us at times. There are young girls who are alone with an unwanted or unplanned pregnancy. They are so lost, seeking care and compassion. How ironic to see dogs who are strays, also bearing a pregnancy. This situation entered my life and, in doing so, ushered in the miracle of Queenie Girl and Jenny.

At the time I first met Queenie, I was employed at a very large residential center for the developmentally disabled. It was a huge expanse of acreage and buildings. Certainly, it was prime territory for stray or feral cats, but hardly advantageous for a stray dog. Many employees across the facility had sightings of her. Reportedly, she was friendly but undernourished and pregnant. My fellow workers found her outside of our building and were able to coax her in with food. It was a sad mystery as to how she got here, probing the questions of whether she got lost or was abandoned. One could see she was not a young dog—perhaps middle-aged and a mixed breed, leaning toward a hound mix. Work restrictions did not allow her to live in the building, so I offered to foster her through the birth and then seek a home for her. How naïve of me to truly believe this would be a collegial effort with my friends. It was all too clear then that an adoption was in the making.

So, as the story unfolded, she was preparing to give birth within a few weeks. A friend of mine, who was a licensed vet technician, was with me to facilitate the delivery. This first-time opportunity to see a litter being born was remarkable, even surreal, and I relished every minute. In the end, Queenie gave birth to four healthy pups. What a mystery to see all four of them with, more than likely, strong genes from dad. All four were a dark brown and even black hue. The last puppy, the so-called runt, was completely black—a black Labrador. Queenie became much healthier, and the pups thrived. In time, they were adopted by fellow workers, and one black lab was left. She was a female, quite striking and extremely affectionate. Time was going by, and a decision had to be made. I saw the writing on the wall and finally acquiesced to keep Queenie and her daughter. I must admit it was a joyful choice with no regrets. The puppy was so gentle and hungry for love. I wanted a name that reflected her sweetness, and so she became Jenny Rebecca. So, mom and child were welcomed into the fold, an assortment of cats, birds, and dogs.

Queenie seemed to enjoy her own company. By nature, she was loving and forbearing, but she was also very stoic. I think she probably developed this trait based on the presumptive rough life she had. She and my shepherd, Lady, were not enamored with each other. Lady was the matriarch and territorial. Queenie was guarded and protective of her space. They occasionally trespassed on each other's space and engaged in a heated dispute. The skirmishes never escalated to the point of physical harm, as I always intervened. They guarded their positioning forcefully, nonetheless. Jenny was an anomaly, as she sought out attention physically to the extreme. She was, by now, a good-sized Labrador retriever still thinking she was a puppy and could squeeze onto your lap. She constantly nuzzled you and leaned against you, whereas sometimes you had to push her away. It saddened me at times not to be able to fulfill all her needs. Something in her personality was flawed or missing, so enough was never enough.

In any event, the two of them were bonded, and I believed they possessed this unseen recognition of their relationship. Not surprisingly, Queenie seemed to do better without the constancy of Jenny, as Jenny would crawl into your soul if necessary to be close.

I was endeared to Queenie and Jenny for many reasons. They were loving creatures, and both had hard times and challenging lives. They were connected by a mutual desire to survive and rose above the kinks in their armor. A brave mother and daughter, without a doubt.

Queenie lived to a ripe old age and succumbed to spinal paralysis. Just as I expected, Jenny, who was battling poorly controlled diabetes, mourned for Queenie and never seemed to be able or want to be this adoring, doting baby. As fate would have it, she developed cancer and passed. When I thought of them, I smiled because I knew they were together, having passed the same year, months apart. I chose to bury both together at my home in a garden. For Queenie, no more wandering, no more abuse. For Jenny, no more need or hunger for love. Home together in bliss, waiting for me...

Randt

There are a plethora of cats that live outdoors; albeit, it is not much of a life, usually fraught with danger, injury, and lack of resources. Humans that care for them have the best of intentions, but not always favorable outcomes. Stray cats tend to be less guarded with caretakers but are still not acceptably acclimated to care. Feral cats, on the other hand, are still not socialized to people and avoid contact out of fear and self-preservation.

In the burgeoning years of my animal ministry, I worked as a veterinary assistant. The hospital was located in a small strip mall, which housed several delis, stores, and fast-food businesses. It goes without saying that there were several outdoor dumpsters that served as a potential resource for scrap food. One of these receptacles was across from the hospital. It would seem plausible that cats would seek out food, perhaps at night when there was less traffic and fewer people.

On one particular day, the veterinarian and I took note of a young black-and-white cat intermittently showing up around the dumpster. The vet thought the cat was young and felt strongly it should be rescued. After setting up a trap/neuter/release trap, it only took a day or two to secure this little one. The veterinarian, whose name was

Randy, had really taken a strong liking to the cat but was not in a position to adopt him (a "he," by the way). Of course, who did she turn to, with every feasible reason as to why I should claim this guy? Well, to be succinct, it didn't take much cajoling, and our guy was hereby named Randt.

Randt was coming to a household of four other cats, so I placed him in a large dog crate with food, water, and litter since he was not totally socialized. It was an invitation for everyone to introduce themselves without any ill feelings. On one particular day, I carefully opened the door of the crate to change the litter, and like quicksilver, Randt slipped through the opening. I realized then that he and I needed to work together to calm him down and integrate him with the others. After several hours of trying to wear him down, I was finally able to pick him up. It was then that I learned a saying that rang true: "Doing something impossible is like trying to corral a bunch of cats!"

I began to recognize that he demonstrated a hybrid personality. He allowed me to pet him once in a while but remained cautious. He didn't engage with the other cats, instead being aloof. It seemed a longing on his part to receive attention and physical closeness, but he was a victim of life's untoward events that scarred him. Randt was guessed to be about two or three years old, so my hope was that we had time to reconcile him to people and his fellow companions.

Randt was unfortunately dealt a medically compromised hand. He was diagnosed with diabetes mellitus, and despite my very best efforts, I could not regulate or control the hypoglycemia. He developed significant nerve damage and, as a result, acquired neuropathy. The nerve damage causes a cat to stand with his weight on his heels instead of his paws. It presents as a "flat-footed" stance.

Randt relegated himself to my bedroom, and he seemed content with a big window to look out of and several beds that he could get into. Not long after, Randt displayed a very mild cough and loss of appetite. I had him examined at the hospital and, sadly, discovered he had cancer throughout his chest.

Time was no longer gifted to him, as his life became more negotiated. I spent time with him every day, and he was so comfortable and calm with my presence. It seemed that the inevitability of his passing somehow brought us closer, and we indeed met each other halfway. As his cancer progressed, I knew his life would be intolerable, and I needed to let him go to spare him not one moment of suffering.

The day he was to be euthanized, I spent time stroking him and speaking to him. Once again, I experienced the most intimate exchange and intersection of spirits with him. He looked into my eyes, and I heard him silently thank me. He gave me his gratitude for my care of him, for our companionship, for my acceptance of his leave, and for the exceptional love between us.

Georgia and Kathryn

It appears to me that animals in need of rescue find the most obscure places for safety. At the same time, I find it no accident that I come across these places where I least expect it. Oh yes, we have animals in and around garbage, empty buildings, in traffic, in bushes and scrubs.

When I find very young kittens, for example, I am distressed that the mother may have abandoned them or was killed. Before I go off on a tangent, let's visit overgrown shrubs, four kittens, and me. This is my recovery of Georgia and Kathryn.

Georgia and Kathryn were found along with two siblings hidden under some bushes. Staff had heard meows coming from that direction but saw no parents. We decided not to touch them or move them in case the mother reappeared. Several days went by with no visible sign of her. We decided, in the best interest of the kittens, to gather them up and bring them to a veterinarian.

The diagnosis was not very promising, as there were significant eye issues. Georgia had corneal ulcers and Kathryn's vision was compromised. The worst of the litter were the other two, who were not as healthy as Georgia and Kathryn, so they went to intensive care for hospice care. A week or so later, they were simply so incapacitated that they lost the fight.

We did eventually see the mother and theorized that she abandoned the litter due to their disfigurement and poor health. We blessed the two little ones and sent them on to their perpetual home of love and peace. Georgia and Kathryn came home with me.

The two girls flourished alongside my other pets. Georgia emerged as a long-haired, striking calico, and Kathryn was white with honey-colored ear tips and tail. Georgia was robust for sure, and Kathryn was quite diminutive.

As I surmised when I adopted them, I would be facing ongoing eye issues with both of them. A great deal of time over the years was spent monitoring and treating them at a veterinary ophthalmology specialist's office. It was discovered that Kathryn had a hole in her optic nerve due to congenital factors. Her vision was significantly impaired, and despite a never-ending regimen of eye drops, medications, and surgeries, she never presented any resistance and remained a very loving, timid cat.

Georgia, on the other hand, suffered from a series of corneal ulcerations—ulcers to be exact. She endured long periods of healing due to the persistence of the ulcers and their chronic emergence. Not surprisingly, she was not the best patient, particularly when she had to wear a plastic cone. In the end, one of her eyes was removed due to severe damage that was beyond repair.

For some unknown reason—just as with people—the girls were not closely knit. Their familial relationship in no way fostered "sisterly" bonding. By nature, Georgia and Kathryn were very sweet and playful, but not with each other. Thankfully, they never engaged in any altercations—just superficial acknowledgment of each other's presence and a peaceful coexistence.

I find that when you have a relationship with a pet, each one has an attribute or personality very special to them. I believed that Georgia and Kathryn were brave and resilient. In spite of their serious health deficits, they never avoided human affection or touch. In fact, they sought it. Georgia rose above her blindness, always jumping on furniture and into windows as if to say, "See, I can see." Kathryn as well remained this precious, cuddly cat, always seeking me out to cuddle with.

We humans and our animal companions often suffer setbacks, injustices, and health challenges. The journey is what tempers us and enhances our strength. The destination is who we are and why we are loved. Nothing can extinguish an indomitable spirit, for it is a beacon.

Georgia and Kathryn were my everlasting light.

Puff

Good things come in small packages. I know this to be true because Puff's diminutive size could not contain his larger than life sweetness and joy. This was my own little powder puff, all furry and cuddly—my dwarf rabbit, Puff.

Puff was such an extraordinary delight. Every time I looked at him, I had to smile. As soon as I got close to his cage, he immediately came over to the door, wiggling and twitching that nose like a hummingbird. He knew it either meant food or playground time.

Time out of his cage was an adventure for a number of reasons. As soon as he was released, he would hop from one spot to another. When he really got his rhythm going, he would literally jump in the air and kick his back legs out of pure joy, pure abandon, and no inhibitions whatsoever. The cats and dog all watched him warily, not quite understanding what he was, but transfixed nonetheless. Puff was totally oblivious, too absorbed in his exhilaration.

Now, Puff always left a token of appreciation, which were droppings—or Puff raisins. This was the one item that the dogs were interested in, so I had to outrace them before they cleaned up the carpet.

Puff was extremely affectionate and bonded to me. Whenever I held him, he buried his head under my chin and wiggled under my shirt neckline. Hugging him was delicious, but amazingly enough, he was the only species to which I was allergic. Once I put him back in his cage, my eyes would get itchy and swell slightly. I got congested and teary—but all in all, a small price to pay for his special embrace.

As Puff got older, he developed digestive problems and sinus issues, common among dwarfs. To break up hairballs from grooming, I had to dispense fresh pineapple juice by mouth with a tiny syringe. Even this he never seemed to mind.

In the end, he developed an abdominal obstruction. He was nearing 10 years old and was a shell of himself. Once this joyful creature was no longer joyful, it was time to release him.

Maybe some people wouldn't understand, but I so deeply, dearly loved Puff. He made my heart and spirit swell with gratitude for allowing me to be a witness to his magical life. I saw him still free and unfettered, leaping and dancing until he could reach the sky.

He taught me how to appreciate the smallest of things and revel in the sheer pleasure and gift of life.

Keep kicking your feet up in your grassy field, Puff! The goodness of this little guy was bigger than life.

Porter

Did you ever notice how we nonchalantly pass by another person without any recognition of them—invisible to our eyes? Are we repelled by their appearance? Have they done something distasteful? Or do we think we are above others? Perhaps it is not intentional—simply self-absorption.

The very same behavior is directed towards animals. There, but not there. A distraction or annoyance.

This was how I met Porter.

There he was in the shelter, in a cage for all intents and purposes out of sight, for no valid reason at all. I was director for only a few weeks when I visited the cat room to assess our adoption potential. Some of the cats hid in the corner of their cage, others stretched their paws through the cage door to implore me, "Take me, take me!" And then there was Porter.

He sat very still and as close to the door as possible, with his two legs stretched out and meeting each other. His position was almost regal, not unlike an Egyptian sphinx. He didn't vocalize or move but kept his eyes fixed on me. It was then that I noticed a very pronounced defect in his eyes—they appeared as though there was layered scar tissue.

I can still remember, to this day, something ethereal and hushed about him. I picked him up and held him, and he sank into my chest as though he had done this a thousand times before. I was somehow able to see through his eyes—a hidden tenderness that was tucked away for safekeeping.

Porter had been rescued as a stray in NYC. He was found wandering around a factory area—namely, one that was the Portland Cement Factory. He was about five years of age, and I scheduled a visit to the veterinary hospital to assess his eyes. It was determined that surgery would be necessary to repair as much of his vision as possible.

The procedure was as successful as they projected, and although not perfect, his vision was improved. It would be fair to say that his vision was comparable to "legally blind."

I decided to have Porter live in my office, which later became the residence of Brook as well. I should have known then that something was afoot—for I was acquiring two new family members.

Porter had been named after the cement company, which simply didn't do justice to his temperament. He was far too dignified, so he was accorded the name Porter.

Porter had a very distinct bond with males. For example, if a gentleman was interviewing with me, Porter would jump on the desk, rub up against the person, even go as far as to climb on their shoulders and wrap himself like a scarf. If that wasn't enough, he would weave in and out of the person's walking path like a figure-eight skater.

Porter was an expert in identifying people who sincerely liked and enjoyed animals.

On a much less positive note, Porter was incontinent. I didn't know it when I first took him in—only to find wet cushions on the chairs. Let the laundry begin, both there and at my home, as Porter did spread the wealth to his beds, towels, etc.!

Porter's favorite thing in the world was cat "junk food" treats. Anytime I went into the kitchen, he took a few steps toward me and glided his feet back and forth in anticipation. Picture him like someone rubbing their hands together in glee. He never missed his treat ritual.

Many animals had passed before, leaving me with Porter and Brook. The two were extremely bonded and ran through the house in chase like two kittens.

Porter lived to see many years and enjoyed all the blessings of a home. He left peacefully at 18, and for his beauty, love, and sweetness, I am forever gifted.

He initiated a transfiguration for all who were in his company. In the light of such, he shined with a blinding light. I found his soul through eyes that couldn't see—and I was the better for it.

My peaceful, serene boy is with me still.

Epilogue

As I close this chronicle and portrait of my "family," I would be remiss in not expressing my gratitude. The privilege of writing a narrative of my life's work is humbling. I thank everyone for taking the time to share my experiences. Most of all, I thank you for who you are. You are my audience and partners in great joy, richness, rewards, and even heartaches.

All the animals I have rescued have been my teachers. Early on, I learned that they share their existence with us. We are intertwined, interconnected, and interdependent. I was moved by an effortless energy to be a guardian and protector. I soon discovered that the price of this responsibility was ever-present reverence and redemption—not only for them but for ourselves as well.

To all animal advocates, your commitment is nothing short of miraculous. You have been endowed with hope, energy, faith, and the promise of continuity. Sometimes, however, it is easy to become lazy or inattentive, and we forget our covenant. Our relationship with our companions becomes a foreclosure on our promises. They give unrivaled love, loyalty, and patience—and ask for the same.

Are we careless with them? Are we selfish with our time? Do we take them for granted? Too often, this happens, and we need a transfusion of responsibility. Keep in mind that at some point, a bill may arrive that you can't pay.

I was deeply moved the first time I heard a song called *"Life is a Church,"* written and performed by David Philips. In my mind's eye, I pictured a Christian church, a temple, a mosque, a synagogue, or just an empty room. In whatever you consider a house of worship, it is so much more. Each one houses an internal creed or state of mind.

Everything in life is a sacrament, and although considered ethereal, blessings are an act of commitment toward the betterment of others. To bless the animals means to live a life of integrity. The blessings we receive are, in turn, passed on to the animals as a gift of our humanity. Their sacraments are rescue and redemption. Their reverence is the spirit and power of our love.

The Christian Holy Trinity illustrates a powerful union. There is, however, another trinity which bridges a connection with all living creatures. No matter what or who you believe in, there lies three entities in one: divine spirit, animals of all species, and mankind.

I am proud to join all who give a piece of themselves to animal ministry every single day. Never forget to be proud of a job well done and a life well lived. No act of kindness is too small or inconsequential.

As you travel this pilgrimage called life, lift your affirmation to heaven and embroider these words on the fabric of your heart: listen for the nightingales on the first summer breeze, hear the whisper and touch of angels every day, smile at the swans' songs, sprinkle fairy dust along the way.

Oh, and by the way—don't forget the French fries!